THE FIRST GLIMP...
OF THE ...

Borman squinted out the w... ...as still only blackness. "On tha... ...y, I can't see squat out there," he said.

"You want us to turn off your lights and check it?" Anders asked, reaching for the interior lighting switches.

Before he could touch them, however, Lovell called out, "Hey, I got the moon!"

"You do?" Anders asked.

"Right below us!" he said, looking through his window.

And indeed, there it was, just visible through Lovell's backward-facing window. The ship had now traveled far enough past the leading edge of the moon that some of the ancient, gray surface stretched beyond the *Apollo*'s nose. The expanse was huge—a ruined, meteor-blasted beach that spread out to the right and left until it spilled over the horizons.

Jim Lovell, the first human being in history to see it, stared transfixed and said nothing.

* * * * * * * *

OTHER BOOKS YOU MAY ENJOY

TO
THE
MOON!

THE TRUE STORY OF THE
AMERICAN HEROES ON THE
APOLLO 8 SPACESHIP

JEFFREY KLUGER

with RUBY SHAMIR

PUFFIN BOOKS

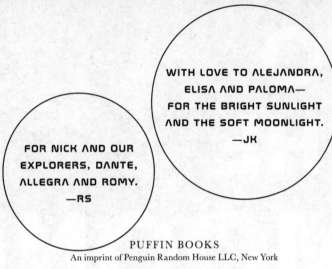

FOR NICK AND OUR
EXPLORERS, DANTE,
ALLEGRA AND ROMY.
—RS

WITH LOVE TO ALEJANDRA,
ELISA AND PALOMA—
FOR THE BRIGHT SUNLIGHT
AND THE SOFT MOONLIGHT.
—JK

PUFFIN BOOKS
An imprint of Penguin Random House LLC, New York

First published in the United States of America by Philomel Books,
an imprint of Penguin Random House LLC, 2018
Published by Puffin Books, an imprint of Penguin Random House LLC, 2019

Visit us online at penguinrandomhouse.com

THE LIBRARY OF CONGRESS HAS CATALOGED THE PHILOMEL BOOKS EDITION AS FOLLOWS:
Names: Kluger, Jeffrey, author. | Shamir, Ruby, author.
Title: To the moon! : the true story of the American heroes on the Apollo 8 spaceship / Jeffrey
Kluger with Ruby Shamir. | Description: New York, NY : Philomel Books, [2018] | Audience:
Age 8–12. | Audience: Grades 4 to 6. | Includes index. | Identifiers: LCCN 2017022353|
ISBN 9781524741013 (hardcover) | ISBN 9781524741020 (e-book) | Subjects: LCSH: Project
Apollo (U.S.)—Juvenile literature. | Space flight to the moon—Juvenile literature. | Apollo 8
(Spacecraft)—Juvenile literature. | Classification: LCC TL789.8.U6 A543253 2018 | DDC
629.45/4—dc23
LC record available at https://lccn.loc.gov/2017022353

Puffin Books ISBN 9781524741037

Printed in the United States of America.

1 3 5 7 9 10 8 6 4 2

Edited by Jill Santopolo. • Design by Ellice M. Lee.
Text set in Baskerville.

• PROLOGUE •

THE LAST THING Frank Borman needed was a phone call when he was trying to fly his spacecraft. No astronaut ever wanted to hear a ringing phone when he was in the middle of a flight, but when the spacecraft was an *Apollo*, any interruption was pretty much unforgivable. The *Apollo* was a beautiful machine—so much bigger, so much sleeker than the *Mercury* and *Gemini* pods that all the other Americans who had ever been in space had flown. But the *Mercury*s and the *Gemini*s had a perfect record: sixteen launches, sixteen splashdowns, and not a crewman lost. The *Apollo*, on the other hand, was already a killer: only eighteen months ago, three very good men had died in the ship before the first one ever got off the launchpad.

So when Borman was trying to fly, he needed to pay complete attention. And now, at precisely the wrong moment, there was a call for him.

In fairness, Borman was not actually midflight when the phone rang. No one had yet taken an *Apollo* into space; that wouldn't happen until the ship was proven fit to fly, which it most certainly had not been. For now, he was merely sitting in the cockpit of the spacecraft on the factory floor at the North

American Aviation plant in Downey, California, where all the new *Apollo*s were being built. If it did fly, Borman's place would be in the left-hand seat—the commander's seat—and that suited him just fine. His crewmates, Jim Lovell and Bill Anders—exceptional men, both—would be in the center and right seats. Lovell and Anders were with him today, in fact, and the work they were doing was every bit as difficult as his own.

This spacecraft, *Apollo 9*, was scheduled to launch in approximately nine months, leaving no wiggle room in the training schedule. That schedule, however, depended on *Apollo*s 7 and 8, the first two crewed flights of the *Apollo* series; both had to get off the ground and bring their crews home whole and well. All three of the flights were supposed to stay in Earth's orbit, and to Borman's way of thinking, that was a shame. It was the boiling summer of 1968, and the world had spent much of the year bleeding from countless wounds: wars, assassinations of American leaders, riots and unrest from Washington to Prague to Paris to Southeast Asia. The Soviet Union and the United States, again and always, were staring each other down in hot spots around the globe as the Cold War raged, while American men died in the war in Vietnam at a rate of more than a thousand each month.

A flight to the moon—which President Kennedy had once promised would happen by 1970—would have been a fine and uplifting achievement right about now. But Kennedy was five years dead by an assassin's bullet and three *Apollo* astronauts were eighteen months dead and the entire lunar project was flailing at best, failing at worst. Most people believed that if

American astronauts reached the moon at all, they wouldn't get there for years.

Still, Borman had his mission, and he and his crew had their ship. And today they were inside it, running their flight drills and doing their best to get the feel of the machine. All the *Apollos* looked the same and were laid out the same, but spacecraft were like aircraft. Pilots could feel their differences—in the give of a seat or the grind of a dial or the stickiness of a switch that had a bit more resistance than it should. Each spacecraft was as particular to each astronaut as a favorite mitt is to a catcher, and you had best know your ship well before you take it into space.

Now, as Borman, Lovell, and Anders lay in their assigned seats in their small cockpit, working to achieve that flier's familiarity, a technician popped his head through the hatch.

"Colonel, there's a phone call for you," he said to Borman.

"Can you take a message?" Borman asked, annoyed at the interruption.

"No, sir. It's Mr. Slayton. He says he has to talk to you."

Borman groaned. Mr. Slayton was Deke Slayton, the head of the astronaut office and the man who assigned all the men to their flights. That power came with the understanding that he could always *un*-assign you to a flight if he chose. When Slayton rang, you took the call.

Borman crawled out of the spacecraft and trotted to the phone. "What is it, Deke?" he asked.

"I've got something important I need to talk to you about, Frank."

"So talk. I'm really busy here."

"Not on the phone. I want you back in Houston now."

"Deke," Borman protested, "I'm right in the middle of—"

"I don't care what you're in the middle of. Be in Houston. Today."

Borman hung up, hurried back to the spacecraft, and told Lovell and Anders about the call, offering only a who-knows shrug when they asked him what it meant. Then he hopped into his T-38 jet and flew alone back to Texas as ordered.

Just a few hours after he was first pulled from his spacecraft, Borman was sitting in Slayton's office. Chris Kraft, Borman noticed with interest, was there as well. Kraft was NASA's director of flight operations; as such, he was Slayton's boss and Borman's boss and almost everyone else's boss, save NASA's top administrators themselves. But today he remained silent and let the chief astronaut talk.

"Frank, we want to change your flight," Slayton said simply.

"All right, Deke . . . ," Borman said tentatively.

Slayton held up his hand. "There's more," he said. "We want to bump you and your crew from *Apollo 9* up to *Apollo 8*. You'll take that spacecraft since it's further along—and you'll fly it to the moon."

Then, as if to make clear that the astounding statement Borman had just heard was really what Slayton meant to say, he put it another way: "We are changing your flight from an Earth orbital mission to a lunar orbital," he said, adding: "The best launch window is December 21. That gives you sixteen weeks to get ready. Do you want the flight?"

Borman said nothing at first, taking in the weight of what Slayton was proposing.

Before Borman could fully gather his thoughts, Kraft spoke up. "It's your call, Frank," he said.

That, all three men knew, was entirely true—and entirely untrue, too. Borman was a soldier, a West Point graduate and an air force fighter pilot. He had never had an opportunity to fight in a hot war, but the space program was a race with the Soviet Union and a critical part of the Cold War. A battlefield assignment—no matter what kind of battlefield—was not something he could possibly turn down.

The way Borman saw it, circumstances might warrant your saying no to a dangerous assignment, and your commanding officer might forgive you for saying no, but if you hadn't signed up to fight, then why did you become a soldier in the first place? And if you hadn't joined the space program to fly to the moon when your boss and your nation and—somewhere in that long chain of command—your president were asking you to, well, maybe you should have chosen a different line of work. The *Apollo* spacecraft might not be up to the job, the flight planners who had the same sixteen weeks to get ready for a mission to the moon might not know exactly what they are doing, and in the end, three more *Apollo* astronauts might wind up dead. But death was always a part of the piloting calculus, and this time would be no different.

"Yes, Deke," Borman said. "I'll take the flight."

"And Lovell and Anders?" Slayton asked.

"They'll take it, too," Borman responded briskly.

"You're sure about them?"

"I'm sure," Borman answered. Then he smiled inwardly. He could only imagine the look on Lovell's and Anders's faces if he had flown back to Downey and told them that they had all been offered the chance to go to the moon before Christmastime and he had answered, *No thanks.*

* * * * * * * *

There was no established way for a man to tell his wife and kids he was going to the moon. A man could tell his family he was going to sea or going to war; men had been doing that for millennia. But the moon? That was a whole new conversation.

When the commander got word that his assignment had been changed from an *Apollo 9* Earth orbit to an *Apollo 8* lunar orbit, he came home and told his wife Susan the news; she looked at him and said, "Okay." He then told his boys, who were seventeen and fifteen; they looked at him and said, "Okay," too. That was the way it went the first time Borman flew into space, three years earlier, and that was the way it had always gone when Borman was given a dangerous assignment. The kids especially didn't realize anything unusual was happening. They had spent their lives on military bases or surrounded by other pilots' and astronauts' families. To them, this was just another part of Dad's day job.

But this time was different, because no other astronaut had ever gone to the moon before, and a moon mission was exactly what the boys' dad had just accepted. Still, the Bormans would find a way to manage this challenge, just as they had managed every difficult challenge they'd faced before. Susan and Frank even had a shorthand for their preferred approach, and it went like this: "The custard is in the oven at three hundred fifty degrees."

Frank would mention the custard when he was requesting combat duty or trying out a dangerous new plane; Susan would mention the custard when they were looking at a new house or sending the boys to a new school. They both took comfort in the little incantation. What the custard meant—with its sense of domestic coziness—was that Susan would tend to the home and the boys, and Frank would tend to the flying. And if they both did that, while taking care not to overstep to the other person's patch, the custard would come out just fine.

But this new challenge, Susan realized, might require something more than the custard. She had been an astronaut's wife for a long time and she realized at a primal level that something about this mission was particularly troubling, something that went beyond the obvious risks most people were considering. Frank wouldn't be landing on the moon; in fact, the spidery lunar module that would be needed for that final step in the moon project hadn't even been fully built yet. But an orbital mission posed its own dark peril.

The most important piece of hardware on an *Apollo* spacecraft was its engine—the big, roaring blunderbuss at the rear of the ship, the machine that some of the more superstitious people in NASA referred to merely as The Engine, the same way they would say The Queen or The President or The Moon itself, with the "The" giving it an almost supernatural specialness. Borman, Lovell and Anders referred to the engine by its brisk, clinical initials: to them it was the SPS, short for Service Propulsion System. The label nicely expressed its job, which was to propel and to serve.

A machine that played so central a role in a lunar mission could not possibly fail. But what if it did? That was the worry. If you were planning to orbit the moon, you would need your SPS to fire at least twice: the first time to slow you down so you'd surrender to the moon's gravity and become a lunar satellite—that was called the Lunar Orbit Insertion, or LOI—and the second time at the end of your visit so you'd speed back up and peel off for Earth—that was called the Trans-Earth Injection, or TEI. If the engine failed the first time, the mission would be wrecked, but the crew might survive, whipping around the moon and coming home. If it failed the second time, the crew would be trapped in lunar orbit. Sealed inside a metal coffin, the astronauts would never come home, but never descend for a conclusive crash into the lunar surface, either. That engine failure would effectively ruin the moon: no one could ever look up at it again and not be aware of the three dead men. They would circle the moon as it circled the Earth, on and on, forever and ever.

So Susan decided to talk to NASA's director of flight operations. Apart from her husband, Chris Kraft was perhaps the only person in the space program with whom she could be herself. He had a sandpaper temperament and a pitiless honesty that Susan found refreshing. And since the NASA families living in the communities around the space center in Houston were a sociable bunch, she figured she'd have a chance to talk with him before long. Sure enough, shortly after Borman got his lunar assignment, Kraft dropped by their house one evening, and Susan seized a private moment.

"Chris, I'd really appreciate it if you'd level with me," she said. "I really want to know what you think their chances are of coming home." It was a straight-up question and she held his eyes, insisting that he give her an equally straight-up answer.

Kraft studied her face. "You really mean that, don't you?" he asked.

"Yes," Susan said, "and you know I do."

Kraft did know. "Okay," he said directly, "how's fifty–fifty?" Susan nodded. She had suspected as much.

ONE

Mid-1961

BEFORE HE COULD venture to the moon, Frank Borman would first have to master the flying machines he'd loved since he was a little boy.

Born in 1928, the only child of Edwin and Marjorie Borman, Frank was supposed to grow up in Gary, Indiana, where his father ran a successful garage business, a point of pride in the early years of the Great Depression when so many other families were struggling. But the trick to living happily in Gary was overlooking the persistent chill and leaden dampness that often settled on the area. Though most Indianans could tolerate the weather, young Frank couldn't. Sinus problems, repeated colds and ear infections kept him out of school so regularly that the family's doctor warned his parents that if the boy didn't get somewhere dry and warm fast, he might grow up with no hearing at all.

So the family abandoned their life in Gary and moved to Tucson, Arizona. Frank promptly got well, thrived in school and took to building and flying model airplanes, then more model airplanes, and then many more still. When he was a senior in high school, the year after the end of World War II—a war in which air power played a major role—he decided that flying real airplanes was what he wanted to do with his life.

The best route to the best planes, he knew, was to get himself accepted to West Point, and from there, to make his way to the air force. The only problem was, by the time he decided he wanted to go to the military academy, it was technically too late for him to apply. But by a stroke of luck, and more than a little finagling, he managed to get on the waiting list and was then accepted. Borman, to his own amazement, was to take his place as a shaven-headed plebe, the military academy word for freshman, in the class of 1950.

As he'd suspected he would, Borman loved every single thing about West Point. He was a hard worker and relished West Point's head-cracking academics and ferocious discipline and the deep camaraderie that came from standing on the lowest rung of an exceedingly hierarchical system.

Unlike a lot of the other plebes, Borman even learned to appreciate the self-control that came from tolerating the hazing at the hands of more senior cadets, though that part was not easy. There was the business of eating in silence with his back perfectly straight and in a full-brace position, or complying uncomplainingly when an upperclassman would unmake a perfectly made bed and have him remake it.

Ultimately, the young cadet became so assimilated to the military life that when his four years at West Point were done, he graduated eighth in his class of 670 people, an accomplishment impressive enough to earn him his longed-for assignment to the air force. Upon graduation, he received orders to report to Nellis Air Force Base in southeastern Nevada, where he would train to fly the F-80 fighter jet, before shipping out sometime in 1951 to combat in the Korean War.

Before he headed to Nellis, he wanted to make sure one very special person would come with him. He asked his longtime love Susan to marry him, and she agreed to become his wife. Borman had achieved precisely the trajectory he had planned for himself. It was all going so right, that maybe he was too cocky or too blind to see how one foolish risk could send it all crashing down.

* * * * * * * *

Nevada's Nellis Air Force Base was exactly what Borman expected it to be: a passable enough place for a young military officer and his new bride to make a home, and an extraordinary place to learn combat flying. And it was clear to all the fliers on the base that their skills would be needed soon.

The men at Nellis were anxious to get into combat in the Korean War, and their training was intensified so that they would be battle-ready in as short a time as possible. Borman, whose star had shone so brightly at West Point, was determined to make his mark as an aviator as well. And that led him to do a very dumb thing.

One afternoon, several months after arriving at Nellis, Borman hopped into an F-80 to run some dive-bombing drills, just to sharpen the skills he would need once he got into combat.

It was a fine way to spend a free hour or two, except on a day when a pilot had a bad head cold.

At the top of a climb, just as Borman was beginning a dive, his head exploded, or felt as if it had. A lightning bolt of pain erupted from somewhere deep between his ears, one that defied the natural response to pain, which is to grab the thing that hurts. But grabbing your head when you're flying an F-80 at six hundred miles per hour is simply not an option.

Instead Borman gritted his teeth, nursed the plane and himself down to the ground and immediately went to see the doctor on the base. The pain now seemed to be localized in one ear; peering inside that ear, the doctor made the lethal little *tsk*ing noise doctors make when they suspect that something is seriously wrong and then discover that the situation is even worse than they'd feared.

"The eardrum," he explained to the young lieutenant, "is made of three separate layers. You've ruptured them all."

Whatever Borman was thinking when he chose to fly on a day when his head was badly clogged was his own affair, the doctor said, but the damage he had done was serious. The ear might or might not heal; either way, the doctor couldn't offer a meaningful prognosis until Borman came back for a follow-up visit in about six weeks. In the meantime, his file would be stamped DNIF, or Duty Not Involving Flying. For a pilot on the rise, those four letters were the worst you could possibly hear.

Borman protested, but the doctor held fast. The young aviator explained that his unit would be shipping out for Korea in less than six weeks; that may well be true, the doctor said, but if so, the unit would be going without him. Ultimately, Borman was indeed left behind, and when he returned to see the doctor six weeks later, the three ruptured layers were still blown.

Borman's prognosis and his grounding persisted for close to a year as he was shipped out to a peaceable posting in the Philippines. It was so peaceable, in fact, that he was able to bring along his wife and their infant son, Frederick, born just weeks before. They would all be assigned a spot in base housing just right for a young family. His new assignment would be director of roads and grounds; effectively, he would be the base's chief of maintenance. There might be a more humiliating title for a grounded flier than one that actually included the word "grounds," but Borman did not care to try to come up with one.

✱ ✱ ✱ ✱ ✱ ✱ ✱ ✱

Life in the Philippines was not merely as bad as Borman had feared it would be, it was vastly worse. He tried every which way to get out of there, but was rejected at every turn.

After one layer of his eardrum finally healed, Borman appealed directly to the squadron commander, Major Charles McGee, an African American pilot who had flown and fought extensively in World War II when the military was racially segregated. A man who had fought for his country despite enduring racial discrimination, Borman thought, was someone to be respected—and someone Borman assumed would play straight with him. He approached McGee and explained that he was absolutely certain that his one-layer eardrum was up to the job of flying, at all altitudes, in all conditions. The problem was, the air force was refusing to give him the chance to go up and find out for sure. If he flew and the eardrum blew again, he understood that he would have to accept a permanent grounding. But if it didn't blow, he could be back in the sky.

McGee agreed it was worth finding out, so he took Borman flying. Borman tolerated the changing pressures and the dizzying swoops with no difficulty and no pain. When they landed, McGee smiled at Borman and told him, "Better go see the doctor again." Before Borman could dart off and do just that, McGee added a warning: "And tell him the truth."

The doctor inspected Borman's ear and offered the usual unremarkable diagnosis—the one layer of the eardrum was still intact but otherwise there had been no improvement. Borman cut him off before he could finish.

"Doc, you might as well know I've been flying with McGee," he said.

The doctor dismissed Borman and called McGee, who told him that yes, what the eager young lieutenant had said was true. The doctor was skeptical—*he* was the medical man after all. But McGee was a flier, and he had spent a good part of a grueling day with another flier, and a fine one. Perhaps, the squadron commander suggested, a man who so badly wanted to serve his country, and had now proven his fitness to do so, ought to have his wings returned to him.

The doctor evidently agreed. Shortly after, the official

notification arrived in the Borman home. "In the case of First Lieutenant Frank Borman," the document read, "subject has been returned to flying status."

✳ ✳ ✳ ✳ ✳ ✳ ✳ ✳

In the decade that followed, Borman pursued his love of flying with a near-consuming fever. He and Susan and their now two young sons—Edwin arrived just nineteen months after Frederick—moved from base to base, hopscotching the US as the needs of the military demanded. By 1961, he and his family were living at Edwards Air Force Base in California and he had at last become the highly accomplished flier he had long wanted to be. But one piece was still missing.

Borman had been too young to fight in World War II and had been grounded before he ever got a chance to get to Korea; now, as a thirty-three-year-old pilot with young children, he knew that his chances of engaging in the combat he'd been training for his entire adult life were rapidly diminishing. If the call to arms against the Soviets came, it would likely not go out to him. There were younger fliers who would surely be sent first. Borman had missed his window.

But if there were hot warriors, as there had been throughout all of humanity's bloody history, there were now cold warriors, too. This was a whole new kind of fighting.

For nearly two decades, since the end of World War II, the United States and the Soviet Union—Russia and its satellite countries in Eastern Europe and Central Asia—had been locked in a competition for world domination. The Americans feared the Russians were an immediate threat to their way of life and the Russians felt the same way about the Americans. Both countries began forging separate alliances with countries on the global chessboard and building up their arsenal of nuclear weapons. Nukes are not run-of-the-mill battlefield bombs, but weapons that could burn up entire cities in a flash. While neither side wanted to actually use the nukes, the threat they posed put any potential for diplomacy on ice, creating a need for this new type of soldier: the cold warrior. Cold warriors drew up the plans and trained the soldiers who might have to fight if the Soviets attacked.

On October 4, 1957, the Soviet Union successfully launched *Sputnik*, the first satellite, into orbit around the Earth. This beach-ball-size uncrewed device set off alarm bells in the halls of power and around kitchen tables all over the United States. Could future satellites spy on us or drop bombs on unsuspecting Americans anywhere? The fear of a Soviet nuclear attack, which had already been instilled in American schoolkids as they practiced hiding under their classroom desks or running to the nearest bomb shelter, suddenly felt terrifyingly closer. The Cold War battlefield moved beyond the clouds and absolute supremacy in the space race became a life-or-death matter. Its heroes—the astronauts who would lead expeditions into space—would be real-life supermen—and at first only men were permitted to apply.

Russia did send the first woman into space in 1963. And at NASA, women scientists and mathematicians were involved in some of the complex number crunching to design these missions.

Women had even taken the tests to be astronauts for NASA and proved exceptionally resilient—tougher than some of the men, in fact—but since they were barred from the air force, NASA refused to allow them into space, either.

The seven Cold Warriors everyone knew best had been hand-selected from the military in 1959, dressed in silver pressure suits, and taught to fly not jets but rockets. These were the soldiers sent off to beat the Soviets in the highest, fastest combat of all: the competition for space. They were the first fighters in a different kind of war, and if you thought that flying rockets didn't count as real combat—that climbing on top of a ninety-five-foot *Atlas* booster full of explosive fuel was not at least as big a risk as flying into battle—well, you didn't know much about calculating odds.

The country's first astronauts had become famous and, by pilots' standards, rich. Now, even before all the original astronauts had flown, the call was going out for a second class of recruits. This time nine of them would be selected, and they would be flying not the little one-man *Mercury* spacecraft, but the two-man *Gemini* and later the three-man *Apollo* spacecraft—and the *Apollo*s were the ships that would go to the moon.

The air force was aggressively encouraging its men to volunteer. In case there was any doubt about that, General Curtis LeMay, the air force chief of staff himself—a short, solid man who had flown bombing missions in both Europe and the Pacific during World War II—summoned the officers who had submitted their applications to NASA for a sit-down in Washington. Borman was among them.

"I'm hearing that some of you think you'll be deserting the air force," he said in his signature growl that could seem unfriendly, mostly because it was. "You're not deserting the air force, and you're not ducking combat. The Cold War is real, real as any war. Go fight it—and make the air force look good."

That was all the invitation and forgiveness Borman needed. Not long after his application went out, he was called in for weeks of grueling physicals and other trials demanded by the space program. He had no fear of passing the flight tests and skills tests and intelligence tests, but the medical tests were another matter. His single-layer eardrum might have been good enough for jets, but he had no idea whether it would be deemed suitable for space. He lived in dread of the moment when the first NASA doctor would examine his ears.

The day for his medical examination arrived, and as soon as one of the NASA doctors stuck a scope inside the damaged ear he emitted a low whistle of disbelief.

"Get a look at this," he called to another doctor, who came over, took the scope and made the whistling noise, too. This little scene was repeated two or three times, until at last the man who appeared to be the head doctor looked through the scope.

"Young man," he asked Borman, "does that ear bother you?"

"No sir it doesn't bother me it doesn't bother me at all," Borman answered with no audible pause between any of his words.

"Well," the doctor replied after a thoughtful moment, "if it doesn't bother you, it doesn't bother me."

And that, to Borman's utter amazement, was that.

Borman went back to Edwards, where he could do nothing but wait for NASA's decision. He did not have to wait long. One morning in the spring of 1962, he received a phone call and learned that the decision had been made: yes, he was going to become an astronaut. He hung up the phone, pumped his fist in triumph and drove straight home to Susan. The moment he walked in the door, she could tell from his face that something very good had happened.

"Well, look," Borman said, suddenly feeling more modest about his news than he expected. "I was selected."

Susan did not have to ask for any more information. She threw her arms around him and hugged him tightly. It was one more reassignment in the life of an air force officer's family—but an assignment like no other.

TWO

1962–1964

THE PEOPLE AT NASA knew how to put on a good show, and how to make it irresistible to the press. The rockets were beautiful, the astronauts were dashing, and their families were charming. If you read all the stories in the newspapers and magazines, you couldn't help but believe that the space agency was showing and telling you everything you needed to know about how it went about its business. But the space agency was also good at keeping a very big secret: half the time their engineers were just making things up as they went along.

Building machines that could carry men safely above the atmosphere was an order of magnitude harder than building the flying machines that could merely carry men through it. Making the spacecraft themselves—the airtight pods that would be cockpit and home for the crew—was actually the easier part, if only because they would require little fuel to maneuver in space and were thus unlikely to blow up while they were still on Earth. The rockets themselves were another matter.

No one with any sense would admit this part of the story to the public or the press, of course, much less to the US Congress, which was providing the funding to keep the agency running. But from the beginning, a certain amount of on-the-fly improvisation was probably inevitable, because NASA's Brainbusters, as they were called, were inventing ways to send humans where they had never been before—to space.

✳ ✳ ✳ ✳ ✳ ✳ ✳ ✳

Frank Borman and the rest of the second astronaut class were welcomed to NASA in 1962, and by that point, the men who ran the agency had done a reasonably good job of figuring out how to make spacecraft and rockets. Americans had flown in space four times now: Al Shepard's and Gus Grissom's two suborbital missions, John Glenn's three-lap romp around the planet, and Scott Carpenter's duplicate three-orbit flight. All of these one-man Mercury missions were triumphs—as long as you didn't look too closely.

Shepard's flight had indeed been flawless. Grissom's almost was, but then the spacecraft splashed down and the hatch blew too early and the astronaut almost drowned before being hauled out of the ocean by a horse collar dangling from a helicopter. Glenn's flight, too, had been fine right until the end, when suddenly it looked like his heat shield—the thick plate of heat-dissipating material that would protect him from the 3,000-degree inferno of reentry—might be loose, which caused a lot of live-TV hand-wringing before the spacecraft at last hissed safely down into the ocean, with Glenn happy and unharmed. Carpenter's flight was the least successful of the four, though the mistakes were more or less of his own making. After faffing around too much with his orbital experiments, he hit his reentry rockets too late, causing him to overshoot his recovery area by 250 miles and requiring the navy to go searching for him.

With the one-man *Mercury* spacecraft having achieved most of its objectives and only a couple of longer-duration missions left to fly, it was now time to roll out the bigger, more sophisticated two-man *Gemini* spacecraft, and to roll out the new astronauts who would fly them.

Americans swooned when the Original Seven astronauts had been unveiled in 1959, but the second crew of pilots, of which Frank Borman was one, was often known simply as the Next Nine.

Though the Next Nine didn't make the same kind of splash as the Original Seven, they still got a lot of the same perks. *Life* magazine paid each of the new men $16,000 per year, an altogether princely sum for pilots who had spent a career earning military pay. *Life* did this to ensure its reporters could slip into the homes of the astronauts and their families and catch glimpses of how each family handled their dad's new extraterrestrial assignment, details the world was hungry to read about. And in its own way, NASA provided, too. When they first got to Houston in September 1962, the nine new astronauts and their young families were told to report to the Shamrock Hilton, a legendary place that advertised itself as "America's Magnificent Hotel." To all appearances, the Shamrock's nearly imperial lobby, massive ballrooms and trapezoidal swimming pool with its three-tier diving board lived up to the hype.

Frank Borman was as dazzled by the place as the other

astronauts, but that didn't mean he was entirely comfortable with it. He and his family had lived modestly at Edwards and they had driven from the air base to Houston in his 1960 Chevy. Just because his job had changed, Borman saw no reason to change his ways. Even a *Life* magazine contract didn't inspire him to begin throwing his money around.

"We can't afford this," Borman whispered to Susan when they walked into the hotel.

But as it turned out, they could. When Borman approached the desk and gave his name, the clerk glanced down at his guest registry and then looked back up, beaming at the man he had just learned was an astronaut. The clerk assured him that the Shamrock was at his disposal for as long as he and his family needed it. It was the least the hotel could do for an American hero.

No matter how glamorous the new lodgings were, Borman would accept them for only so long, especially since he had thus far done nothing to earn the praise of the hotel's staff. As quickly as possible, he and Susan went looking for a piece of land on which they could build a home. The house, which they built in the El Lago neighborhood, near other astronauts and their families, would be an extravagance, but the Bormans decided that their two boys finally deserved a real home.

✳ ✳ ✳ ✳ ✳ ✳ ✳ ✳

If any of the Next Nine were under the impression that an astronaut's job involved little more than learning to fly a spaceship, they were quickly set straight. The two-man *Gemini* hadn't even been fully built yet, the *Titan* booster that would carry it into orbit had not yet been man-rated, and a lot of work needed to be done before anyone would take any rides aboard either of them.

Yes, there would be plenty of basic training in centrifuges and simulators. The astronauts would spend endless hours in classrooms, studying orbital mechanics, lifting bodies and zero gravity, or "zero-g" navigation, to say nothing of survival training on the ocean and in the deserts and anywhere else an errant landing might deposit a pair of astronauts. But that still left extra hours in the week, so all the new recruits would be assigned a specialty, thus giving them a direct hand in developing the hardware, software and flight procedures on which they would be banking their lives. The responsibility for matching up the man and the job went to the no-nonsense Donald Kent "Deke" Slayton, the same man who would call Frank Borman a few years later and ask him if he wanted to be the first spacecraft commander to fly to the moon.

Slayton was impressed by Frank Borman the moment he met him, and what he liked most were the traits that were not unlike Slayton's own. He liked Borman's absence of flash, his ability to block out distractions, his sheer doggedness.

Slayton gave the young astronaut a number of assignments, the most important of which was to investigate the *Gemini*'s intended rocket, the *Titan*, and make sure the rocket could fly without killing the men riding aboard it. Borman didn't know a thing about boosters—or at least he didn't know more than any new astronaut knew—but he knew that you couldn't get into space without them.

A spacecraft depends on powerful rockets loaded with combustible fuel to shoot past the atmosphere—at least 100 miles up—to orbit successfully. And it needs to go fast, because air can push on the ship and slow it down the same way it does if you stick your hand out the window of a moving car. The spacecraft speeds out of the atmosphere going an unimaginable 17,500 miles per hour, which is why you can orbit the entire Earth once in less than ninety minutes. If you're too slow or too low when you blast off, you'll just fall back through the atmosphere to the ground, pulled down by the force of gravity, like a ball tossed into the air. But before you can go anywhere at all—fast or slow—you first have to get off the ground, and Borman had been suspicious of the *Titan* almost from the start.

The problem went to the very heart of the rocket's design. The simplest boosters had one main engine, but the *Titan* had two. Two engines meant two chances for something to go wrong, and that could be especially dangerous on the launchpad. If the rocket started to lift off and both engines quit, it wouldn't go anywhere. But the engines were mounted side by side, so if only one quit, the *Titan* would rise up and then go badly awry, flying first sideways and then down to an unsurvivable crash.

That scenario, Borman figured, was a risk that needed addressing. He dug into the *Titan*'s technical manuals and manufacturing schematics, and although he saw some fail-safes that ought to prevent a one-engine ignition from happening, he was not impressed by what the design ought to do. All that mattered was what the engine *would* do, and something in his gut told him this rocket was trouble.

So Borman went to see the rocket for himself, making it a point to be at Cape Kennedy for the next *Titan* test launch. When he got there, he met the engineers who had designed and built the booster, and he raised his concern with them.

The lead engineer waved off Borman's worry. "It can't happen," he said.

"Anything can happen," Borman answered.

The engineer shook his head. "There could never be a failure mode in which just one barrel fires," he said flatly. "It's simply not the way the system works."

Borman let the matter go but decided to stay in the Cape for a few days and wait for the next *Titan* test. When the day for the new test arrived, he and the engineers crowded into the blockhouse, Mission Control for the launch. The rocket's systems were checked, the countdown clock marched toward zero, and the launch director called, "Ignition."

And on every screen what every man in the room saw was a single engine roaring with fire and a second engine remaining cold and dark and silent. The rocket strained to lift itself into the air.

"Shutdown!" the launch director called just before the crippled machine actually did leave the pad. That part at least worked as it was supposed to, and the *Titan* settled back to the ground.

Borman looked at the nearest engineer, and the engineer—to his credit—met his eyes. The young astronaut had been right after all: *Anything can happen.*

✳ ✳ ✳ ✳ ✳ ✳ ✳

The first flight of the *Gemini* spacecraft, on April 8, 1964, was a lot less momentous than it might have been. Designed to be a test cruise of the *Titan* booster and the *Gemini* itself, it would carry no astronauts into space. The ship would orbit the Earth three times, but wouldn't even reenter the atmosphere under the parachute that would someday be needed to return a crew safely. Instead, it would simply burn up on the way down. And to ensure that no bits of debris would endanger anyone on the ground below or reveal too much about the spacecraft's design, should parts of it rain down behind the Soviet Union's Iron Curtain, NASA engineers drilled holes in the heat shield. The four-ton ship would be effectively vaporized by the intense heat it would face upon reentry into the Earth's atmosphere.

When *Gemini 1* accomplished its modest goals, NASA was elated. No American had been in space for almost a year, and the US was itching to be back in the game. After one more uncrewed flight, *Gemini 3* would at last take off and carry its history-making two-man crew into space. Beyond that mission, there would be up to ten more, with a *Gemini* due to be launched as frequently as once every seven or eight weeks. That meant a lot of seats for a lot of astronauts, and although one flight might seem to be as good as any other, the whispered word among all the pilots was simple: *Whatever you do, don't get stuck with* Gemini 7.

The problem with *Gemini 7*, as every astronaut knew, was that the mission apparently had but a single purpose: to torment its two-man crew for fourteen straight days and nights.

Ever since the *Gemini* was first unveiled, there had been a lot of talk coming out of NASA about the grandeur of the new spacecraft. It would be so much bigger and so much more sophisticated than the *Mercury* ships. There was plenty of truth to that: the *Mercury* had been little more than a pod filled with instruments, with a single man stuffed inside. The pilot could fire his thrusters to waggle the ship this way and that. He could fiddle with his altitude and orient himself for reentry, though the computer could do that perfectly well if he allowed it to. He could also fire his retro-rockets to bring himself home, but the automatic system was more than capable of handling that job for him, too. Even the *Mercury*'s window was little more than a porthole over the astronaut's head, one he could see out of only if he craned his neck backward. For a pilot with any self-respect, the *Mercury* was as much carnival ride as spacecraft.

But the *Gemini*—the *Gemini* would be different. The astronauts flying it wouldn't be going to the moon, but it would be as close to a dress rehearsal for lunar flights as was possible.

The *Gemini* would have a proper cockpit, with two men sitting upright and side by side in seats they liked to call couches, probably to fool themselves into thinking they felt more comfortable than they were. Each would have a window directly in front of him that could be used to sight-fly the ship, like a real pilot should. *Gemini* would be capable of rendezvousing and docking with other spacecraft, linking up in space the way an *Apollo* command module and a spidery lunar lander would have to do one day. The astronauts could fire their thrusters and raise their orbit to eight hundred or nine hundred or even one thousand miles up, blowing past the 176-mile altitude record astronaut Wally Schirra had set on his six-orbit *Mercury* flight.

And on at least a few of the missions, an astronaut would open his hatch and climb outside and walk—actually *walk*—in space, becoming, in effect, a human spacecraft hanging in the void outside a mechanical spacecraft.

The Gemini missions would do all that and more, but they would test another machine as well: the human machine. By NASA's calculations, the maximum length of a lunar voyage would last two weeks, far more time than any human being had ever dared spend in space. Before you could entrust your body to the mercies of the moon, you had to run the experiment much closer to home. If you were orbiting the Earth and your weightless blood began to pool in your brain, or your heart forgot how to work after too much time in microgravity, you could fire your rockets and be back on the ground and in the arms of a medic within a couple of hours.

Somewhere in the middle of all those dazzling Gemini missions, then, there would have to be one long, gritty, grind of a mission, one in which two astronauts would be sealed inside their ship, sent into space, and told they would be allowed to return home when fourteen days—or 224 orbits or 336 hours— had been completed. No rendezvous or altitude records or spacewalking for these men, though they would see plenty of sunrises and sunsets as they circled the planet over and over again. They wouldn't conduct experiments, or at least not many. Instead, they would *be* the experiment.

This was the mission that every astronaut hoped to duck. Slayton, who was making flight assignments, called Borman into his office to inform him he had drawn the short straw: Borman had been assigned to *Gemini 7*. The chief astronaut did offer one consolation, however: on this flight he would be the commander, seated in the left-hand couch. In the right-hand seat would be navy man Jim Lovell, who, it seemed, had drawn a shorter straw still.

Borman and Lovell, as Slayton had ordered, promptly set about training for *Gemini 7*, the worst flight anyone could imagine—until it turned out to be something else entirely.

THREE

Summer and Fall 1965

THE NEWLY NAMED crew of *Gemini 7* learned a lot of things while they were training for their first flight into space, but the least pleasant of them was that no NASA doctor ever seemed to consider a week complete unless he got the chance to mess with an astronaut. To the medical men, astronauts offered one of the greatest controlled experiments ever devised. They were a small group of hand-selected, exquisitely trained men, representatives of a species purpose-built to live in the radiation-shielded, temperature-controlled environment of Earth, where all we know is the regular old pull of gravity, one g. Then those same men would be removed from that little incubator and hurled into a completely different environment for hours or days or even longer, while the entire science community studied how the men responded to such extreme otherworldliness.

Better still, the flying lab rats didn't even have to be coaxed to volunteer. Astronauts clamored for the job—competed fiercely for it, in fact. They would practically do it for free. It was all the doctors could do to contain themselves.

The first astronaut class had suffered seemingly endless

testing, and it became an open secret that the medical examinations they had endured in order to be selected had been exhaustive, invasive and flat-out humiliating. When the men were presented to the public at their first press conference in Washington, DC, in 1959, they could have been forgiven if they had hobbled to the rostrum. At one point in the carefully stage-managed session, a reporter wanted to know which test they liked least.

The other reporters laughed, the NASA administrators squirmed and the astronauts looked at one another and smiled. This was a question made for Wally Schirra.

Early on, Schirra had established himself as the bad boy and practical joker of the first astronaut class. On the dais, in 1959, Wally seemed prepared to answer the awkward question, but John Glenn stole the moment.

"That's a real tough one," he said. "It's rather difficult to pick one, because if you figure out how many openings there are on a human body and how far you can go in any one of them . . ."

Glenn trailed off and then looked at the questioner with a nearly Wally-like twinkle. "Now you answer which one would be the toughest for *you*."

The room howled. Glenn blushed. Then he sat back in his chair.

Even Schirra was forced to concede the match. "I think he's answered for all of us," he said.

Now, in early 1965, with the flight of *Gemini 7* in the planning stages, the doctors had the most promising lab specimens of all in Frank Borman and Jim Lovell, and they planned to make the most of them. Borman and Lovell were made to repeat many of the awful exercises they had endured to get into the program in the first place—all the blood draws and dye injections, the electrified needles and centrifuge runs, the electroencephalograms and electrocardiograms and electromyograms. New tests would give the medics a baseline to measure how the astronauts held up during an unheard-of two weeks in space.

Of particular and nearly obsessive interest to the doctors was the matter of calcium retention. Put a man in space for too long and his skeleton—which suddenly has little work to do, since it no longer needs to support the body against gravity—will stop wasting time keeping itself strong. Calcium in food, which would ordinarily go to maintaining and strengthening bones, will pass right through the body.

The experiment developed by the medical men was almost absurd in its thoroughness. The two astronauts would be required to bag and save every drop of urine and every gram of feces they produced in the nine days before the flight; do the same during the fourteen days aloft and for the four additional days that would follow; and turn it all over to the NASA doctors. Even that wouldn't provide enough data, however, so tears and sweat would also be collected before the mission. Further, Borman and Lovell would be required to stand in a wading pool in nothing but their skivvies while distilled water was poured over them, after which every drop would be collected and sampled for calcium. During and after the flight, the medics would demand that the astronauts save and turn in their underwear—unwashed, please—at the end of every day so that it could be sampled for the sweat it had spent eighteen or so hours wicking up from the men's most personal places.

Blood pressure, balance, heart rate, respiration and vision would be tested as well, both before the flight and repeatedly while the astronauts were in orbit. But the vision test presented a problem. In a tiny two-man cockpit, it would be impossible to position an eye chart far enough away for it to be effective. Even if it were possible, the doctors wondered if the men would run the test honestly and tell the truth if their vision was going soft, or if they would lie to avoid the risk of being told to come home early.

The plan to use an eye chart was abandoned. Instead, on a vacant plot of land forty miles north of Laredo, Texas, NASA groundsmen would flatten and rake eight squares of terrain—2,000 feet long to a side each—and cover them with either white Styrofoam or dark turf. The astronauts would have to describe the pattern of the alternating dark-light squares as they flew overhead, a pattern that could be switched up every time the spacecraft passed over Laredo. Let the flyboys try to cheat on *that* one.

And then finally the doctors went too far. "If you're going to try staying in space for two weeks," one of the doctors said, "it's probably smart to simulate it on Earth first."

"We're spending half our time in simulators as it is," Borman answered.

"But for only a few hours at a time," the doctor said.

"We could always book more," Lovell said as Borman nodded in agreement.

"Right," the doctor responded. "But what we're talking about is simulating the whole thing, the whole two weeks—beginning to end. Just to play it safe."

Borman was incredulous. "You want us to spend fourteen days in straight-up seats? In a one-g environment—with no bathroom breaks?"

"Well, yes," the doctor said.

"Are you out of your *minds*?" Borman barked.

The doctors had no answer for that, though they surely would have offered one if they did. At the prerogative of the mission commander, that experiment was scrapped.

✱ ✱ ✱ ✱ ✱ ✱ ✱

If anything made the notion of spending two weeks in the corrugated can that was *Gemini 7* more tolerable for Borman, it was the prospect of going aloft with his fellow astronaut, Jim Lovell.

Borman had met Lovell during the astronaut selection process, when they and a group of other applicants were undergoing physicals at Brooks Air Force Base in San Antonio, and he liked him from the start. For one thing, there was Lovell's temperament. The military was full of growling types and joker types, and, Borman had to admit, hard-driven, hard-charging grinds like himself. What it lacked were the easygoing, uncomplicated types, the men who never got rattled. They stayed cool not because they didn't take things seriously or failed to understand the odds, but because it simply was not in their natures to run hot.

"If you can't get along with Lovell," went the popular wisdom in the astronaut corps, "you can't get along with anyone."

Just as appealing to Borman was Lovell's background, which was so much like his own. He could forgive Lovell's choice of the Naval Academy over West Point because, as any West Pointer would tell you, every man is entitled to one major mistake in his life. But Lovell, just like Borman, had had to scrap his way into his school of choice and later, into NASA's astronaut program after an overblown medical technicality made him ineligible. Lovell took his initial rejection as a temporary answer, one that would be set right in the future. In 1962, when NASA was screening its second class of astronaut candidates, it was.

✷ ✷ ✷ ✷ ✷ ✷ ✷

Before *Gemini 7* could get its chance to go to space, *Gemini 6* would have to fly. *Gemini*s *3*, *4*, and *5* had been almost complete successes, with the high point being Ed White's *Gemini 4* space walk, the first ever for an American astronaut. The flight of *Gemini 6* would begin with a launch less than two months before Borman and Lovell's scheduled liftoff in December 1965. Both men planned to be on hand to watch the two-man *Gemini 6* crew—Wally Schirra and rookie Tom Stafford—take off.

Like all space launches, countdown and liftoff would occur under the watchful eye of the engineers in the blockhouse at Cape Kennedy, but once the engine bells at the bottom of the rocket climbed higher than the launch tower next to the launchpad, Mission Control in Houston would take over. Cape Kennedy,

Florida, was the perfect launch site for two big reasons: First, if any rocket that launched from there crashed, it would fall harmlessly into the Atlantic Ocean, rather than near a population center. Second, it was nearly as close to the equator as you can get in the Continental US, which means your rocket gets extra speed for free.

The equator is the widest part of the Earth, with a circumference of 24,000 miles. The Earth takes twenty-four hours to rotate, which means that if you're standing at any point on the equator, you're always moving at 1,000 miles per hour, even if you can't feel it. If you go to near the top of the Earth, just 3.8 miles from the North Pole, and draw a circle so that every point on that circle is also 3.8 miles from the North Pole, you have a different circumference of only twenty-four miles. But the spot on which you're standing will take the same twenty-four hours to make one complete rotation, which means you're only moving at one mile per hour. If you launch a rocket to orbit the Earth from that point, you get that extra one mile per hour added to your speed for free. If you launch it from the equator, you get 1,000 miles per hour for free. That makes a huge difference since rockets have to be very big and powerful to achieve the speed of 17,500 miles per hour, which allows a spacecraft to shoot into orbit. It helps a lot when you get a 1,000-mile-per-hour head start.

October 25 broke as a perfectly clear morning in coastal Florida. The day was unusually hot for so late in the year, but that didn't stop the tens of thousands of campers and spectators from lining the beaches surrounding the launch site, and it didn't stop the big three television networks and all the major newspapers from converging, too.

This wasn't just the biggest show in town, nor simply a chance to witness history. Viewers gathered at the launch site and around their television sets to cheer on fellow Americans as they spectacularly defied gravity and departed our Earthly home, not to mention showed up the Soviets, who were racing to do the same. Americans tuned in to these launches as a balm, too, to remember all the ways the United States could lead, even as unsettling news was beginning to pile up day by day about the war in Vietnam and problems on the home front.

Swarms of people and press had attended the one-man *Mercury* launches, and the same was true for the first three *Gemini*s. But *Gemini 6* drew easily one of the biggest crowds yet, mostly because there would be two launches that day, barely ninety minutes apart, instead of the usual one. First up, the *Atlas* rocket would punch an uncrewed *Agena* spacecraft into the sky; after that, the *Titan* rocket with a *Gemini* spacecraft perched on top and Schirra and Stafford tucked inside would blast off. For the gawkers, that meant twice the number of countdowns and twice the level of thrills. For the morbid—and the media—it meant twice the chance that something would go disastrously wrong.

If everything went exactly as NASA had scripted it, the astronauts would spend a day chasing the *Agena* down in space and then park the nose of the *Gemini* into the collar of the *Agena*, locking them together like a single vehicle, a sequence they had practiced on Earth umpteen times.

NASA's moon-landing plans called for exactly this kind of maneuver: someday, a lunar excursion module, or LEM, with two men aboard, would lift off from the surface of the moon and dock with a command module—an eleven-foot-tall cone that contained the cockpit where the astronauts lived—with one man aboard, that was orbiting overhead. Once all three men were safely inside the command module, they would jettison the LEM and all three would come home. The US had never managed such a rendezvous and docking feat even in Earth orbit, and the Soviet Union hadn't, either. This would be a good chance to practice the maneuver, check a box in the pre–moon mission to-do list, and tweak the Russians as well. The entire Gemini 6 mission would take just two days, but the space race would be transformed after it was over.

So far, things looked promising. With just over two minutes to go, the TV cameras switched away from the correspondents to a view of the *Atlas-Agena* on the pad. A digital clock super-imposed on the screen counted down the seconds; precisely at zero, the engine of the uncrewed rocket lit.

"Liftoff right on the button, right on the hour," Walter Cronkite, the CBS News anchor, enthused. "There goes that fiery boom of the *Atlas*."

While Cronkite admired these massive machines and the astronauts who flew them, most everyone in America admired Walter Cronkite. Sure, you could read about the launch or any of the day's events in your local newspaper the next morning, but nothing beat the live broadcast on one of the three major television networks viewers could choose from. And Walter

Cronkite, at once warm and serious, a reassuring storyteller who never strayed from the facts, was the visitor Americans trusted most to be invited into their living rooms night after night to convey the latest on anything worth knowing. Once again, he'd have an important story to tell.

But then, just under five minutes into the flight, at the moment the *Agena* was supposed to have separated from the booster, the tracking station on the Canary Islands reported that it had lost the signal from the *Agena*, with data screens going blank both there and in Mission Control in Houston. What took the place of the healthy vital signs of a spacecraft speeding into orbit was the worst thing possible: a radar signal from a land-based station that was receiving five scattered reflections spreading across the sky in what could only suggest an explosion.

It was fatal. The tens of thousands of people who had camped on the beaches to watch the two liftoffs might not have understood that, but the people in the VIP stands—at least the ones who worked for NASA—did. Schirra and Stafford, strapped into their rocket ship to nowhere, knew it, too. And so did every man at every console in the launch control center.

It would be a full fifty minutes before the Canary Islands tracking station confirmed the death of the *Agena* and, by extension, the scrubbing of the *Gemini 6* launch with the simple words "No joy, no joy." By then, Borman and Lovell, who had been watching from the viewing stand, had quit for the launch control center and found the predicted gloom. But they also found the beginnings of a mad bit of improvisational genius.

Chris Kraft was huddled with a few of his top engineers when one gave voice to what a few others were already thinking.

"Suppose we use a *Gemini* as a target instead of an *Agena*?" one asked. For those who didn't quite understand his point, he added, "Launch *Gemini 7* first and make it the target for *6*."

"You're out of your mind," Kraft said immediately. "That can't be done." But even as he spoke the words, it was becoming clear to him and everyone else in the room that it could indeed be done. In truth, it was practically begging to be done.

A joint mission would mean four men in orbit at once, placed there by a space program that only four years ago had struggled to launch even a single man on a suborbital high jump for a five-minute glimpse of space.

Once the two *Gemini*s were in orbit, there could be no docking between them; the ships weren't built that way. But it was the rendezvous part of the mission that was the hardest and most important: two pickup-truck-size vehicles that were moving at 17,500 miles per hour would have to find one another in millions of cubic miles of near-Earth space and then approach to within just inches of each other. The astronauts would get so close they'd be able to recognize one another's faces in the windows; achieving that kind of precision would be a big step forward for the space program.

Launching a dual mission would not mean moving up the date of the *Gemini 7* launch, not least because Borman and Lovell still had a month of training to go. But it would mean sending the two spacecraft up in reverse order. Once *Gemini 7* launched and was in orbit, the ground team would have eight to ten days to roll out *Gemini 6* and get it into space while a few days remained in the fourteen-day mission of *Gemini 7*.

Despite himself, Kraft had to admit that he was warming to the makeshift madness of the thing. NASA would have to resolve a number of problems first: how to modify a global tracking web built to follow one spacecraft so that it could keep track of two; whether the navigational algorithms could be written in time for the computers that would help guide the two spacecraft. But those were the kinds of problems Brainbusters had always been paid to solve, and these were the kinds of made-up, on-the-fly missions that astronauts always hoped to participate in. Kraft, ever and always a Brainbuster, gave the go-ahead: four men in two different spacecraft would for the first time ever meet in space.

FOUR

December 4, 1965

THE PRECISE MOMENT when a *Titan* rocket ignited underneath an astronaut for the first time always came as a surprise. The pilots all thought they were prepared for it, because the people who trained them had sworn they would be. But when the moment finally happened, the astronauts realized that the trainers had no idea what they were talking about.

The first thing no one mentioned was the *glug-glug-glugg*ing sound that began thirty seconds before the engines even lit. More than 120,000 gallons of two different kinds of hot-tempered fuel were sloshing around in the ten-story booster, and if the rocket was going to go anywhere at all, those volatile chemicals would have to flow and mix. And since the fuel pumps were high up in the booster, right beneath the *Gemini* spacecraft perched on top, the sound—which was like a giant bathtub draining—was impossible to miss and impossible to feel terribly good about.

The astronauts also weren't prepared for the way the booster would sway in the wind while it was waiting to take off. The higher up the stack, the worse the sway, which meant it was worst of all for the two men tucked inside the *Gemini* at the very top. And though the astronauts had spent hours in centrifuges getting used to the seven-g force of gravity they would be pulling after they at last took off, making it feel like invisible hands pressing on their chests and limbs, constricting their movement and even their breathing, they didn't fully appreciate how quickly they would feel the grip of that force, almost the moment the rocket jumped off the pad. That was yet another feature of the *Titan*'s ballistic missile pedigree: a weapon that's taking to the sky to defend the homeland from attack can hardly afford to dawdle while getting into the air.

Most of all, there was the noise of ignition. During the endless simulations, the trainers never bothered trying to re-create it, because even the best sim could not reproduce the cannon roar of a *Titan*'s engines. You had to be inside the cannon itself, which is exactly where an astronaut would be on launch day, and at no other time. Without the help of the radio, it would be hopeless to try to talk to the man in the next seat; the closed helmet muffled the astronauts' voices and the sound of the rocket drowned everything else out. Even with the helmet microphone positioned just an inch from the mouth, astronauts still had to shout to be heard.

At 2:30 p.m. on December 4, 1965—precisely the date and time the NASA flight controllers had aimed for, even with all the improvisational planning they'd done in the past six weeks—Frank Borman and Jim Lovell experienced the unimaginably ferocious blast of a *Titan* rocket for the first time.

"We're on our way, Frank!" Lovell yelled to Borman.

Borman, rattling about in the left-hand seat, said something or other in response, but it was hopelessly lost in the noise, even to his own ears. He tried again, this time settling for a quick, affirmative, "Right!"

"Communications are a little noisy from the spacecraft," said NASA commentator Paul Haney, understating the reality by a considerable factor for the tens of millions of people watching on television.

The days leading up to the launch had been predictably busy, not only for Borman and Lovell, but also for their understudies, Ed White and Mike Collins. White and Collins were the backup crew, and both men had to be ready to fly on very short notice.

Borman was especially pleased that his own understudy was Commander Ed White. Borman had been a military man and an astronaut long enough to know how to establish a camaraderie with the men around him. But camaraderie and abiding friendship were different things, and though he shared the first with a great many people, he shared the second most powerfully with White. The Bormans and the Whites lived across the street from each other, and the families got along unusually well. Susan and Ed's wife, Pat, were closer than nearly any other pair of women in the astronaut wives sorority, and the Borman boys—Fred and Ed—got on well with the White children, Edwin and Bonnie Lynn, with admirably little teasing directed at the one girl from the three boys. The four friends and their children often spent weekends together, and the two astronauts would take the opportunity to fish and talk space—or fish and talk about anything other than space.

On *Gemini 7*'s launch day, Borman, Lovell and their two backups awoke at 7:00 a.m. Both crews prepared meticulously for liftoff; before Borman and Lovell even entered the capsule, White and Collins had spent an hour there, checking out the systems and making sure it was ready to fly. Just before noon, the two second-stringers climbed out and the two primary astronauts were loaded into the spacecraft and strapped into their seats. Then the twin hatches—one over each astronaut's head—were closed.

The hours before ignition moved exceedingly slowly. Borman was glad that he and Lovell had eaten a big breakfast that morning; the meal was the last good one they would have for a while. Plenty of fine-sounding food was stowed aboard the spacecraft for the fourteen days they would spend aloft—chicken and vegetables, shrimp cocktail, beef and gravy, butterscotch pudding, packaged fruits—but all of it had been shrink-wrapped or freeze-dried to within an inch of its life, and all of it would have to be eaten with a spoon from a plastic pouch that had to be opened with a pair of surgical scissors. There would also be fruitcake—lots and lots of fruitcake—packaged like sausage links in a long necklace stowed behind Lovell's seat. It was energy-dense and high in calories, but nobody pretended it would taste any better in space than it did on Earth.

But now, as their rocket climbed and the g-forces built, pressing them down into their seats, food was not remotely on the astronauts' minds. At two minutes and thirty-nine seconds into the launch, exactly on schedule, the first stage of the rocket shut down and fell away, flinging Borman and Lovell forward in their seat restraints. A moment later, the second stage lit, slamming them back again in their seats. The higher the gravitational pull, or g's, the more a body weighs. The g-forces climbed on schedule to four and then five, six, and seven, meaning that within seconds the two men, who weighed the astronaut average of about 155 pounds on Earth, clocked in at more than 1,100 pounds on the balance scale of gravitational physics. If, in a matter of moments, you suddenly weigh seven times your starting weight, it becomes very hard to move.

And then, five minutes and forty seconds after they left the coast of Florida—less time than it would have taken to walk from the launchpad to the Cape Kennedy commissary—their engine cut off, their spacecraft entered orbit, and the astronauts suddenly weighed nothing at all. Around them, bits of dust and the odd screw or bolt that were inevitably left behind in even the most painstakingly prepared spacecraft floated lazily in the air. Like all first-timers, Borman and Lovell poked at the drifting flotsam, grinned at it, and then grinned at each other.

"*Gemini 7*, you are go!" called up the capsule communicator—or capcom—at Mission Control in Houston.

"Roger," Borman answered. "Thank you."

Borman and Lovell, who now formally and forever had joined the small fraternity of men who had flown in space, simply grinned again.

✳ ✳ ✳ ✳ ✳ ✳ ✳

It didn't take long before *Gemini 7* became precisely the 330-hour grind it was advertised to be. For two weeks, a pair of full-grown men would be locked in an enclosure with no more habitable volume than the front seat of a Volkswagen Beetle and even less room overhead than the Beetle offers. The two astronauts quickly learned that they could extend and stretch their legs, but only if they bent their upper bodies. Or they could stretch their upper bodies, but only if they bent their legs. Doing both at once was impossible. There was also a lot of instrument noise, the whirring and ticking and whooshing of the thrusters and the ventilators that were the very heartbeat of the ship. Borman and Lovell might have found the noise reassuring, except that it never, ever stopped.

Even sleeping wasn't easy, with the capcom's chatter added to that constant background sound. That back-and-forth with the ground didn't stop, either, because NASA rules required that at least one astronaut remain awake at all times, and polite whispering was nothing like silence when your fellow pilot sat just inches away from you.

The menu, meanwhile, was just as bad as they had suspected it would be. Foods that had to be rehydrated with a water gun never achieved the right texture: dry, powdery bites alternated with sticky, watery ones, and no single bite struck the proper balance. The fruits packed with sugary syrup were a little better, as was the punch. The fruitcake was . . . fruitcake.

And then there was the business of the space suits. Humans are uniquely designed for life on Earth. We need oxygen to breathe; a precise, narrow temperature range; and the air around us to exert an imperceptible pressure on our bodies, which keeps our blood from actually boiling. Alter the details even a little, and humans can't survive. A space suit is actually a kind of spacecraft. It provides astronauts with temperature control, breathable air, some minimal radiation protection and, most important, a sealed environment, maintaining a safe air pressure.

But on *Gemini 7*, the space suits themselves became impossible. For a fourteen-day flight, the usual fighter pilot pressure suits and the hard shell helmets simply would not do, so NASA had ordered up lighter, softer suits with cloth helmets that zipped open and shut, could be folded back like a jacket hood, and could, at the very least, get the astronauts safely back to the ground in the event of an emergency at liftoff or reentry to the Earth's atmosphere. But these "get-me-down" suits were clingy and almost unbearably hot. Peeling them off would leave the crew in far more comfortable long johns, but NASA didn't like that idea, since get-me-down suits can't actually get you down if you're not wearing them.

So Borman sweltered in his suit, turning his air-circulation knob to its coolest setting, which helped little, while Lovell, over the course of the first few days, slipped slowly out of his. First he eased the suit down around his shoulders (surely NASA wouldn't object to that). Then he lowered it to his waist, and finally, he freed all but his lower legs. Both men reported their discomfort to the ground, and over the next six days, the question of suits or skivvies rose up the chain of command. The capcom passed it on to the flight director, who passed it on to Chris Kraft, who passed it on to the deputy administrator in Washington, who consulted with the lead flight surgeon, who reported that, yes, the biomedical readings he was getting from the ship showed that Lovell—who by now was fooling no one with his secretly vanishing space suit—had healthier blood pressure and pulse readings than those for poor suited Borman. The word thus came back down the chain that it was the opinion of NASA brass that the advantages of flying without suits outweighed advantages of wearing them, and the men of *Gemini 7* were officially cleared to fly in their underwear.

As the first day unfolded into the first week and the unshowered, unshaven astronauts grew grittier and riper, there was the ongoing problem of how a man preserves his last scrap of privacy—to say nothing of dignity—in a spacecraft with no proper toilet facilities. Urinating in space was not a problem, and the doctors, it turned out, decided they would need only occasional samples. This meant the men could usually relieve themselves into a tube and then vent it through a small port on the exterior of the spacecraft, where it would instantly burst into a shower of glittery crystals, a phenomenon Wally Schirra had dubbed the Constellation Urion.

But urinating wasn't the only problem, and the remaining one required plastic bags and disposable wipes and a lot of maneuvering if an astronaut was to take care of the matter properly. The other fellow, meanwhile, either pretended not to notice or acknowledged that he very much did notice and asked what in the world the man next to him had eaten before he left the ground. Lovell made peace with the fact that he would have to make use of the awful NASA fecal bags; for him it was a small price to pay for the privilege of flying in space.

Borman had his own solution to the problem: he simply wouldn't confront it. In his view, if a man couldn't control his own bowels, he couldn't control anything at all, and if that meant controlling them for fourteen straight days, that's what he would do. Through sheer will and orneriness, Borman made it through the first week and then through an eighth day. Partly out of self-interest, even Lovell was beginning to root for him. But no man can hold out forever.

"Jim," Borman said on Day Nine, "I think this is it."

"Frank, you have only five more days left to go here," Lovell joked. But five days was five too many, and Borman, who believed that any obstacle could be overcome, learned in a new and very primal way that, no, not all of them can be.

✳ ✳ ✳ ✳ ✳ ✳ ✳ ✳

After more than a week in space, Borman and Lovell were justifiably bored, and the novelty of the planned rendezvous with Wally Schirra and Tom Stafford flying up to meet them in their *Gemini 6* occupied their thoughts. They would have to wait a few days longer than originally planned due to a big technical problem in the *Titan* rocket caused by a tiny, nickel-size plastic dustcover blocking a valve deep in the ten-story stack. But finally, on December 14 at 10:28 a.m., *Gemini 6* left Earth.

"The clock has started," Schirra shouted as the *Titan*'s engines lit. "It's a real one!"

"Trajectory is real good," said the capcom in Houston.

"Roger, she looks like a dream," Schirra said.

"You're go from here, *Gemini 6*."

"You got a big fat go from us," Schirra answered. "It looks great!"

Borman and Lovell, passing directly over coastal Florida, initially saw nothing, as overcast skies completely obscured Cape Kennedy. But when Schirra and Stafford punched through the cloud cover, Borman spotted the white thread of the condensation trail following the rocket and the firefly light of the *Titan* itself.

"I got it; I got the contrail!" Borman called.

Craning his neck to peek through Borman's window, Lovell spotted it, too. "It's going to be getting crowded up here," he said.

It would take four orbits for that two-spacecraft crowd to form. And for nearly six hours, the Earth-based radar-tracking that had been minding only *Gemini 7* would have to mind *6* as well. Meanwhile, engineers in Mission Control would be working along with the astronauts and the computers to pinpoint two tiny machines in the enormity of the Earth's orbital space and then draw them closer and closer together.

Borman and Lovell donned their hated suits, leaving only the hooded helmets unzipped and open. NASA rules would never allow two spacecraft to come even remotely within collision distance without ensuring that the astronauts would be protected if a crash cracked the ship's hull.

For several days, *Gemini 7* had been flying through its orbits in a slow tumble as a means of conserving fuel for planned and unplanned maneuvers. A spacecraft in orbit was not like a jet in flight, which would usually follow its nose wherever it was pointed, because when floating in zero gravity, it didn't matter if the astronauts' ship was upside down or on its side. As long as speed and altitude remained in the right balance, physics guaranteed a stable orbit, no matter which way a spacecraft pitched or yawed or rolled. Now, however, Borman took hold of his thrusters and stabilized *Gemini 7* in a proper, nose-first orientation. It was the only safe way to conduct a rendezvous; almost as important, at least to a pilot, it was the only respectable way.

Gemini 6, with its full tank of thruster fuel and its plan to spend only a little more than twenty-four hours in space, would do the real work in the orbital tango for two. While *6* went hunting and *7* awaited its visitor, the radar told both ships that they were indeed drawing close, but so far neither could see the other.

When the two craft were still more than sixty miles apart, with *Gemini 6* in the shadow of an Earthly night and *Gemini 7* in the full light of day, Schirra turned off the cockpit lights, the better to see the target he was chasing. It was Stafford who saw what they were looking for first, as the bright sunlight reflected off the back half of *Gemini 7*, which, unlike the dark front half, was painted a brilliant white.

"Hey, I think I got it," he called over an open mic so that Houston could hear him, too. "That's *Seven*, Wally."

"Negative," Houston responded, relying on the radar readings flickering on a screen, rather than the human eyeballs out in space.

"Yes," Schirra replied, now seeing the pinprick of light as well.

"It's either Sirius or *Seven*," Stafford allowed, conceding that he might be seeing only the brightest star visible in the sky at that moment.

But it wasn't a star. Schirra tweaked his thrusters. The ships closed to a handful of miles, then a few thousand yards and then a few hundred.

Soon the four men were close enough to see one another through the half-moon windows. While Schirra and Stafford were still crisp and clean-shaven after a shower they had taken just that morning, Borman and Lovell were uncombed and bearded.

"Hello there!" Schirra called out, beaming. Then he directed his attention to the ground. "We're in formation with *Seven*. Everything is great here!"

Borman smiled back but chose to stick to business. Orbital rendezvous might be a critical step in the long march to the moon, but it was also an exceedingly tricky one and could go badly awry at any second. "I'm reading about ten degrees, one hundred and ten degrees," he said, updating Houston on the orientation of his ship in two of its three axes.

Schirra was in no mood to be serious yet. "We're all sitting up here playing bridge together," he said.

Knowing the rendezvous would last only a few orbits, however, Schirra soon got to work. There was a lot to get done, including the inspection of each ship by the crew of the other. No American astronaut had ever seen his spacecraft from outside while in flight, save Ed White during his brief space walk on *Gemini 4*, and he spent most of the walk concentrating on keeping himself upright. Now NASA would get a chance to eyeball its machines as they orbited, and the astronauts had been instructed to look for anomalies, like gapped welds or seams, that might not show in the telemetry, but could be disastrous all the same. Inspecting the ships after they returned was much less reliable, because there was no way of knowing if damage had occurred during reentry.

Schirra was surprised to see a tangle of cords and cables streaming from the back of *Gemini 7*, the remains of the electrical network that had connected it to the *Titan* before explosive bolts blew the two machines apart.

"You guys are really showing a lot of droop on those wires hanging there," Schirra radioed.

"You have one, too," Borman answered, making it clear on the air-to-ground loop that he wasn't the only commander in the sky today whose ship was not quite parade-ready. "It really belted around there when you were firing your thrusters."

Small American flags and the words "United States" were painted on all *Gemini* spacecraft, but when earlier *Gemini*s returned from orbit, much of the flag and lettering had been burned away. No one had ever been sure if the fire of liftoff or the fire of reentry had scoured them so badly.

"The flag and the letters are visible," Lovell now said, inspecting *6* as it hovered nearby. "Looks like they're seared as much at launch as they are when you come back."

"Your blue field is practically burned off," Stafford said.

For more than three orbits, the two ships kept their stations—approaching, retreating, flying circles around each other. The remarkable performance offered reassuring proof that the choreography needed for a trip to the moon was indeed possible. In Mission Control, the men at their consoles savored the moment and even waved small flags. Typically, this sort of celebration was reserved for the very end of a mission, but Chris Kraft permitted it to take place early this time.

Finally, on the first and only day of the mission of *Gemini 6* and the eleventh day in the mission of *Gemini 7*, the station-keeping that had been maintained for hours broke off. Schirra backed away, opened the distance he had worked so hard to close, and began easing down to a lower orbit, preparing to reenter Earth's atmosphere.

When the two ships were no longer in sight of each other, Schirra radioed a final transmission—an urgent one, from the sound of it.

"*Gemini 7*, this is *Gemini 6*. We have an object, looks like a satellite going from north to south, probably in a polar orbit," Schirra reported. "He has a very low trajectory and a very high climbing ratio. Looks like he might be going to reenter soon. Stand by, just let me try to pick up that thing."

A moment later, crackling across the radio in both *Gemini 7* and Mission Control, just nine days before Christmas of 1965, there came a tinny chorus of "Jingle Bells." It was performed live, on a harmonica and small set of bells, contraband that Schirra, ever the joker, had carried aboard his ship.

After he was done, Schirra said proudly, "That was live, 7, not tape."

And then, all business once more, he peeled off and prepared to bring his spacecraft home.

"Really good job, Frank and Jim," he said. "We'll see you on the beach."

* * * * * * * *

Less than an hour later, *Gemini 6* splashed down in the North Atlantic and was recovered by the aircraft carrier USS *Wasp*. Three days after that, *Gemini 7* followed. Its fuel was spent, its power was flickering, and trash was stuffed behind the seats, the only stowage area the spacecraft had. Borman and Lovell—unsteady, exhausted, sorely in need of a very long shower and a very long sleep—waved and smiled gamely as they arrived on the deck of the carrier.

The two astronauts were no better off than their utterly spent spacecraft, but two grueling weeks had come and gone, the men had survived, and the rendezvous had been achieved. And Borman, who had been making a quiet bet with himself, was delighted to learn that when all the course plotting was done, *Gemini 7* had splashed down closer to the *Wasp* than Schirra and his *Gemini 6*.

FIVE

January 1967

GUS GRISSOM, ONE of the Original Seven astronauts, sneaked forbidden food into a spacecraft twice in his life as an astronaut. The first time was a joke; the second time was a forewarning.

The time it was a joke, the contraband was a corned beef sandwich, which Wally Schirra had bought two days earlier at Wolfie's Restaurant and Sandwich Shop in Cocoa Beach. The rapidly aging sandwich smelled terrible, and although it didn't taste bad, it did release a small starburst of floating crumbs in the *Gemini 3* spacecraft the minute Grissom bit into it. So he wrapped it back up and put it away. When the astronauts came home, the NASA contingent that expected mild misbehavior from its astronauts—which was most of NASA—had a good laugh over the prank. The contingent that fretted over even the tiniest deviation from protocol scowled, reminding all the astronauts that a mere bread crumb could snag in a switch or foul a filter and thus cause a cascade of problems that could lead to disaster.

The second time Grissom sneaked forbidden food inside a

cockpit was January 22, 1967. That time the spacecraft was the new, three-man *Apollo* command module. Grissom's ship was not in orbit, but on the floor of the North American Aviation plant in Downey, California, where the *Apollo*s were getting built. And that time, the food was a lemon.

Grissom and his crewmates, Ed White and Roger Chaffee, had been spending a lot of time in their *Apollo 1* in preparation for their February 21, 1967 liftoff. It would be the first flight for the new *Apollo*, and by all appearances, the astronauts would be flying a sweet ship—the most robust, most capable spacecraft NASA and its contractors had ever built. But the appearances were entirely misleading.

To the pilots, the *Apollo* felt like a slapdash machine. It was temperamental, error-prone, and impossible to work with for more than a little while before something broke down. Then a simulation would have to be halted while technicians crawled inside to fool with a faulty communications system or a dead instrument panel or a life-support component that might fail harmlessly on the ground but would kill the crew if it behaved the same way in space. Repairs were made as needed, but they were patchwork affairs—work-arounds and fixes made on top of earlier fixes, rather than the harder work of ripping out the offending systems, redesigning them and reinstalling them only when they worked right. The *Mercury* and *Gemini* spacecraft had had their design problems, but they were glitches in ships that from the beginning looked and felt sound. The *Apollo*s— perhaps because of their complexity, or perhaps because of the rush to get astronauts on the moon before 1970, the year

President Kennedy had set for the moon shot—never earned that confidence.

A disgusted Grissom would complain to the technicians, and then he'd complain to the technicians' bosses, and then he'd complain to the NASA bosses. They would all confer among themselves and promise Gus that they would fix the problem, but still the junkyard spaceship got no better. So one day Grissom decided to make his point a different way. After another long day of trying to make the *Apollo* work the way it was supposed to, he climbed out of the ship and left a lemon perched atop it before walking silently away.

That Gus, the engineers said to one another with indulgent smiles. *Always a little prickly.*

But Grissom had a right to be a lot more than prickly. After the joint flight of *Gemini*s 6 and 7, the space program had been moving along at just the clip NASA had planned. Between the December day when Borman and Lovell splashed down in the North Atlantic and the following November, five more *Gemini*s had flown, one every other month, finishing up with Lovell returning to space as the commander of *Gemini 12*. Lovell had been joined by Buzz Aldrin, a promising rookie from the third astronaut class, and the mission had been a confidence-boosting finale for *Gemini*. Now all of the program's most difficult goals—space walk, rendezvous, docking—had been performed both confidently and competently.

Well before that final spacecraft in the *Gemini* line returned to Earth, manufacturers had begun cutting metal for the *Apollo* line. Both the *Mercury*s and *Gemini*s had been built by McDonnell

Aircraft in St. Louis, and NASA liked the people there just fine. They knew what the space agency needed, delivered what had been ordered, and understood that although they might own the factory and employ the workers, NASA was both the customer and the boss.

But McDonnell couldn't come along for *Apollo*. A venture this big paid factory owners well, and they would in turn hire a lot of workers from the local community. There were plenty of other manufacturers in cities all around the country, and they would all want to know why St. Louis kept finding NASA's favor again and again.

So this time the work went to North American Aviation in Downey, California. When the contract was signed, that seemed like a perfectly suitable choice, but when the work started coming in, it seemed like something else entirely. For starters, there were the folks in what the company called the human-factors division.

Test pilots thought of a man and his plane as two discrete things. One was a deeply dumb machine that was built to do what it was told; the other was a brilliant aerialist whose job it was to tell the machine what to do. But North American Aviation didn't see things that way. Man and machine were but two parts of the same system, and the engineers in the Downey offices believed it was their responsibility to make sure that they performed together properly.

Straight off, that presented problems, particularly for the astronauts themselves. The first pilot to bump up against North American's new—and unwelcome—way of doing business was Frank Borman when he went off to work in the Apollo program, serving on-site in Downey as pilot liaison, and thus helping to shape the ship he and the other astronauts would be flying next.

One day, early in his time there, Borman hopped into the Apollo simulator to give it a trial spin. He was deeply displeased at what he saw.

Trying out the hand controller that fired the simulated thrusters, he realized that the engineers had designed it upside down. When he pulled back on the handle, the *Apollo*'s nose pointed down; when he pushed forward on it, the ship pointed up. That was exactly the opposite of the intuitive way airplanes work—and the way the *Gemini* spacecraft did, too.

He summoned an engineer and pointed with dissatisfaction at the offending handle. "You've got the polarity on this thing reversed," he said, speaking as politely as he could, since the unsuspecting man would surely be embarrassed. "It goes down when you pull up and up when you push down."

"Oh no, that's the way we're going to fly it," the engineer responded brightly. "It makes rendezvousing easier. When you pull back on the stick, the nose goes down, but the target will seem to go up. This way it'll be like you're flying the target, not the spacecraft."

Borman was speechless. First there was the man's presumptuous use of the word "we"—as if there were any question about exactly who would be flying the spacecraft. More important, there was his apparent ignorance about how the astronauts who would be sitting in the cockpit did their work.

"You've got pilots who have been flying jets," he said, just containing himself, "and that's not the way they do it."

"That's the way our human-factors people say we should do it," the man replied, seeming unmoved.

Now Borman was genuinely angry. "Well, that may be the way *you're* going to do it, sitting on your rear as an engineer," he snapped. "But that's not the way *we're* going to do it."

Borman was doing precisely the job he was assigned to do: stop nonsense before it found its way from the brain of an engineer to the metal innards of a spacecraft. In his next call to Houston, he reported how the factory fellows wanted to design the backward thruster. Half an hour after the call, the handle was fixed.

✴ ✴ ✴ ✴ ✴ ✴ ✴ ✴

A mere simulator, however, was not remotely the biggest problem in the *Apollo* factory. Everywhere in the production process, it seemed, rules were being flouted and speed was taking priority over safety. A lot of the North American engineers had learned their craft in the so-called black programs—the classified programs—of the military, which mostly involved building uncrewed vehicles, particularly satellites and missiles. It was hard work, performed to fine tolerances, but none of it involved designing systems that would have to keep a man alive. Their missiles, in particular, didn't even have to work terribly long or terribly well; all they had to do was fly from silo to target and blow up when they were supposed to.

Word of quality control errors in the *Apollo* spacecraft came back to NASA headquarters with disturbing regularity, and the matter eventually found its way up to Chris Kraft, who sent his own quiet representative to the floor at Downey, a Brainbuster who could take a machine apart with his eyes and put it back together in his head so that the redesigned product was almost always better than the original. The report Kraft got back was bleak.

"This hardware is not very good," his Brainbuster reported. "The cabling is being stepped on when they work on the spacecraft. There's no protection for it. The people are not very good at checking this thing out. They're not very good at trying to maintain some semblance of the fact that a human being is going to be in this machine. I'm telling you, it's not good."

But NASA was racing against John Kennedy's fast-approaching deadline and a cranky Congress that was growing increasingly reluctant to fund a moon program at the same time it was pouring money into a widening war in Vietnam. The choice for the space agency seemed to be fly now or wait for perfect hardware and fly never. So despite the dismal reports and complaints from astronauts on the ground at Downey, the work went on and the spacecraft got built. To Kraft and others, their only answer was to pick a crew that inspired complete confidence, one that should be able to handle whatever their troubled spacecraft might throw at them.

Grissom was one of only a handful of men who had been in space twice. He had piloted both the *Mercury* and *Gemini*, and both times he had flown an early iteration of the spacecraft and helped wring out its problems. White had flown once, on *Gemini 4* in 1965, when he made his historic space walk and displayed a remarkable steeliness throughout. The walk looked like grand fun, with pictures showing the white-suited White silhouetted against the blue of Earth and the black of space. But the twenty-three minutes outside the ship had in fact been brutal, a constant struggle against zero-g physics that made maneuvering vastly more difficult than it looked. Even getting safely back inside had proved harrowing: White's hatch had refused to close for a full five minutes. In the end, he had to rely on sheer muscle to yank it shut, exerting himself so much that he fogged his visor completely. Chaffee, the rookie, might not have traveled in space yet, but his experience as a navy pilot proved he was coolheaded when all manner of forces were conspiring to kill him.

As a crew, the three astronauts tried to appear optimistic about their upcoming space mission, but they had no illusions about the jalopy of a ship NASA was handing them. As their launch date drew near, the space agency arranged photo sessions of the astronauts with a model of the *Apollo* spacecraft.

In one photograph that was never circulated to reporters, Grissom, White and Chaffee showed their true feelings about their spacecraft: they posed with their heads bowed and hands held together in prayer. Then, to make sure their message got delivered to the right people, they inscribed it to Harrison "Stormy" Storms, the North American engineer who oversaw the Apollo project. Like the rest of the top people at North American, Storms was well aware that astronauts on the factory floor were regularly making calls to NASA to report yet another problem in the *Apollo* spacecraft.

"Stormy," the inscription read, "this time we're not calling Houston!"

✳ ✳ ✳ ✳ ✳ ✳ ✳ ✳

On January 27, 1967—five days after Grissom made the statement with his lemon and less than a month before the planned launch of *Apollo 1*—NASA planned to conduct what was known as a plugs-out test. The exercise would begin when a fully suited crew climbed inside their spacecraft, which was already on the pad and mounted on top of its *Saturn 1B* booster rocket. With the spacecraft operating on its own internal power system, the crew and the controllers would perform a dress rehearsal of the launch sequence.

Two more steps would ensure as much launch-day authenticity as possible. The first involved the *Apollo*'s atmosphere, an environment with high internal pressure, which was made up of 100-percent oxygen, as it would be in orbit, instead of the 33-percent-oxygen, 77-percent-nitrogen mix of Earth's atmosphere. Since humans need only the oxygen to stay alive, designers decided not to outfit the spacecraft with tanks of inert nitrogen, since that would merely add weight. If anyone was concerned about the fact that fire loves oxygen—especially pure, high-pressure oxygen—that concern did not cause NASA to halt the test.

The second authentic condition involved the hatch, which,

once the astronauts were on their backs and in their seats, was directly behind them, over White's head. In the event of an emergency, Grissom, White and Chaffee would be best served by a hatch they could open in a hurry. That would allow them to tumble out of the ship onto the floor of the white room, the little work space at the end of a swing arm at the top of the gantry tower. The white room surrounded the *Apollo* when the ship was on the pad, and swung back out of the way before liftoff. An easy-open hatch, however, would not be suitable for a cockpit with so much internal pressure. For that, engineers designed a double hatch—an inner one and outer one—and sealed it with multiple latches. If a pad emergency occurred, the man in the center seat would open the latches with a ratchet and then detach the inner hatch, pull it in and lay it down on the floor. Only then could he open the outer hatch. The commander, in the left-hand seat, would assist if needed. The *Apollo 1* astronauts had practiced this sequence many times, and no matter how hard or efficiently they worked, it took time.

The night before the plugs-out test, Wally Schirra, who was Grissom's backup for this mission, went out to the launch-pad with Grissom and spent some time inside the spacecraft, running a few final tests. When he climbed out, he shook his head.

"I don't know," he said to Grissom. "There's nothing I can point to, but something about this ship just doesn't ring right."

It was a damning judgment for a pilot to deliver, suggesting a vehicle that didn't have discrete, fixable problems, but sweeping systemic ones.

And then Schirra added a warning: "If you have any problems, I'd get out."

The plugs-out test at last began at 2:50 p.m., after the crew had settled into their seats and the double hatch had been closed and sealed. The exercise ran slowly and haltingly. The day's most nettlesome problem was one that had occurred in earlier tests, too: balky communications. White and Chaffee could make out the transmissions coming through their headsets, but only through a storm of static and with a lot of dropped words. Grissom's communications line, for reasons the engineers couldn't seem to discover, was even worse.

Before the exercise began, Deke Slayton had offered to climb into the ship along with the crew and spend the entirety of the test period in the lower equipment bay—the small workspace beneath the foot of the couches—to see if he could solve the communications problem. But the plugs-out test was supposed to be as authentic as possible, and since there wouldn't be four men jammed into the three-man ship on launch day, there wouldn't be four men today, either. Instead, Slayton stayed in the launch control center at the Cape, listening as best he could to the garbled communications coming down from the ship.

At 6:20 p.m., an exhausted crew and the exhausted ground teams working at both Cape Kennedy in Florida and Mission Control in Houston got a short break as the simulated countdown went into what was supposed to be a ten-minute hold while the communications breakdown and other glitches were addressed. Kraft, who had been shuttling back and forth between Mission Control in Houston and his nearby office as the countdown started and stopped throughout the afternoon, was now back at his console at the rear of the control room, listening to both the chatter on the ground and the transmissions from the spacecraft.

"How are we going to get to the moon if we can't even talk between three buildings?" Grissom groused at just a few seconds shy of 6:30 p.m. It was one of the rare moments his voice got through clearly.

"They can't hear a thing you're sayin'," White said, his tone bemused.

One minute and fourteen seconds later, the people on the ground did hear something the crew was saying. What they heard was Chaffee shouting, "Hey!"

Next they heard White screaming: "Fire! We've got a fire in the cockpit!"

Then they heard Chaffee shouting: "We have a bad fire!"

And finally they heard Chaffee again, this time screaming: "We're burning up!"

In the white room, the technicians could see frenzied motion through the spacecraft windows. They also saw the flickering light of what was unmistakably a fire.

"Get them out of there!" yelled Donald Babbitt, the pad leader and the chief of the white room. The men around him leapt toward the spacecraft and began wrestling frantically with the hatch. Intense heat radiating from the metal hull forced them to turn their faces to avoid the full power of it.

As the noise and frenzy in the white room increased, the

transmission from the spacecraft became ominously still. Now the voices in the headsets of the men in the control rooms were filled only with the words of the launch controllers themselves—shouting questions to one another at the Cape, staying silent in Houston, where they could do nothing.

"Crew egress!" called the lead test conductor in the launch, following the book and telling the crew to do what they could not possibly do, which was to get out of a spacecraft that had just become a furnace.

"Blow the hatch!" shouted a communications technician nearby. "Why don't they blow the hatch?"

In the white room, one more voice rang out, though no one ever knew whose it was. "Clear the level!" the person called. He was using the agreed-upon language to order all of the people outside the ship to back away—or, if possible, to run away—because the spacecraft was in danger of exploding.

Moments later, the *Apollo* gave off a sound and a blast of air like a bomb, showering the white room with flaming debris and setting fire to loose papers on clipboards and desks. Inside the spacecraft, the fire rushed toward the freedom of the opening, completely engulfing the astronauts. There would be no surviving that; the crew was lost.

Kraft heard every word the dying men said. Slayton—who was sitting at a console, not folded up in the equipment bay of the burning ship—heard it all, too, as did every other man in two control centers. But no one would ever be able to agree on exactly what the astronauts' final words were. Even when recordings of the last few seconds of the men's lives were played, different people remembered hearing different things that the tape didn't capture, which was entirely possible given the unreliability of the communication system.

What many of the men insisted they heard, even though the tape didn't capture it, was one of the astronauts—a professional pilot to the last, a man who knew that as long as you are able to communicate with your flight controllers, you must keep them apprised of the condition of your ship—say as levelly as the circumstances would allow, "I'm reporting a bad fire." The report would be duly noted.

NASA announced the death of the men within the hour, and the networks preempted Friday evening programming with regular reports on the accident at the Cape. The space agency reassured the public that Grissom, White and Chaffee had died almost instantly; though only a small consolation, that was still a mercy. But the official story wasn't true: the three men had lived for a long time as these things go—at least twenty-one seconds, judging by the biometric readings and the activity in the ship that the technicians in the white room had seen through the windows, as well as the data recorded by the spacecraft's motion detectors.

For twenty-one seconds, the astronauts knew what was happening to them and fought to save themselves. To anyone at NASA who had been paying attention, the deaths of Grissom, Chaffee and White were not accidents but inevitabilities— equal parts tragedy and disgrace.

✳ ✳ ✳ ✳ ✳ ✳ ✳ ✳

Gene Kranz, one of NASA's top flight directors, had become one of the most recognized workhorses at the main console in Mission Control. On January 27, the night of the *Apollo 1* plugs-out test, however, Kranz had left the space center early, having gone home for a long-overdue dinner out he'd promised his wife, Marta, who had recently had their third child and was looking forward to a free evening. As he was getting ready, he heard a pounding at the front door. Expecting the babysitter, he frowned at the excessive noise. Still half-dressed, he hurried downstairs and opened the door to see his neighbor, Jim Hannigan, a deputy director of the space center's lunar module division.

"There's been an accident at the Cape," Hannigan said without preamble. "I heard it on the radio. They think the crew is dead."

Kranz tore upstairs, got back into his work clothes and told Marta what he knew. Then he ran out to his car and raced to the campus of NASA's Manned Spacecraft Center. When an out-of-breath Kranz at last entered Mission Control, the scene there chilled him.

At the center console was Kraft, talking in low tones to the flight surgeon at the Cape. Near him was John Hodge, chief of the flight control division. They both looked grim, but nowhere near as much as the pale and shaken younger men at the other consoles. Kranz had flown in combat, and both he and Hodge had worked in test flight, and so both men knew what death looked like.

The junior men in the room had had no such training, no such toughening. Kranz and the other senior figures in the room put the younger men back to work, instructing them to secure their consoles so that every switch and dial remained in exactly the position it was when the fire struck. Somewhere in those thousands of settings might be critical information that would be needed in the investigation to follow—and there would surely be an investigation.

✱ ✱ ✱ ✱ ✱ ✱ ✱ ✱

The weekend that followed the fire was nearly unbearable, not least because most of the Mission Control team had nothing to do until Monday except think about what had happened at the Cape on Friday. But when Monday morning finally arrived, the controllers—bleary-eyed or not, sleepless or not—were expected back at work. When they got there, Kranz was ready for them. He and Hodge called a meeting in the main auditorium in Building 30 on the Manned Spacecraft Center grounds, and attendance was mandatory.

When the controllers took their seats, Hodge spoke first. He talked about what had been learned over the past couple of days; thus far, only a little was known about either the fire's source or the extensive underlying problems in the spacecraft. He announced the names of the men who had initially been assigned to the investigation team, and he talked a bit about how much time would be needed until flights could resume. He conceded that he had no idea if the long-standing deadline for a lunar landing was realistic anymore, but he assured his audience that the NASA administrators would make every effort to come as close as possible to landing on the moon by 1970. Then he turned the stage over to his colleague.

Kranz had spent his weekend thinking hard and getting angry, and he wasn't about to waste an opportunity to drive home a lesson that had come at a tragically high cost. Too often in the previous months, he told the silent controllers, potential problems had been dismissed with a casual that-can't-happen wave. *Maybe the ship had a balky breaker, but it would never cause a fuel cell to fail in flight. Maybe those new pyrotechnics were a little temperamental, but they could never cause a parachute to fail to deploy. And as for pumping pure oxygen into the cockpit, it had never caused any problems before, had it?*

But what if it did? What would you do then? These were the critical questions no one had been raising. It was not good enough to ask what would you accept. Instead, you had to ask what action you would take today to prevent the failure from ever happening. The answer you gave should always satisfy one final question: what is the very best thing to do in this situation?

Kranz made it very clear to the men in the Houston auditorium that the best thing to do was not what had been done in the months leading up to the deaths on Friday. Not a person in the room—himself included—had been tough enough. Every one of them had seen one or more of the problems the *Apollo* spacecraft had been having; everyone had heard the stories about the wreck that was rolling off the lines at North American Aviation. And not one of them had stepped forward and spoken up.

"We had the opportunity to call it off," Kranz said sharply. "We had the opportunity to say, 'This isn't right. Let's shut it down.' And none of us did."

With enough smarts and enough skill, Kranz told them, no mission ever had a reason to fail. It might have problems; it might not achieve every one of its goals. But failure, in all its abject awfulness, cannot be on the menu of possibilities.

"From this day forward," he said, "we will stand for doing everything right, literally being perfect and competent."

Kranz turned to the blackboard behind him and wrote the words "tough and competent." Then he turned back to his young charges.

"I want every one of you to go back to your offices and write those words on the top of your own blackboards," he ordered. "You are not to erase them until we've put a man on the moon."

With that, he put down his chalk, turned on his heel and left the stage. The lesson was over.

* * * * * * * *

The news of the deaths of the three astronauts came to Frank Borman the same way it had come to Gene Kranz: with a knock at the door. Borman, Susan and their boys were staying at a friend's cabin on a lake in Huntsville, Texas, and they were just starting into a long weekend that would at last give Borman a break from the Apollo race. The quest to get the ship off the pad only three months after the last *Gemini* spacecraft flew had been exhausting, and the prelaunch stretch to come promised only to be worse.

The knock on the cabin door that Friday evening was not remotely expected. Borman opened the door to find a Texas Ranger or highway patrolman—he couldn't tell exactly which.

"Colonel Borman?" the officer asked.

"That's me," Borman said.

"I have word from the space center. You're to call Mr. Slayton immediately."

Borman thanked the man and hurried to the phone. He knew even before Slayton answered that the news could not possibly be good, but what the chief astronaut told him was far worse than he had imagined. Borman closed his eyes and felt his stomach drop out; for a moment he could say nothing at all. He would grieve for Grissom and Chaffee, but he would bleed for his friend Ed White. Borman did not give his friendship easily, and now he barely knew what to do with the loss.

He found his voice. "How did it happen, Deke? What went wrong?"

"We don't know," Slayton said. "But you're on the team that's going to investigate this thing. Be at the Cape tomorrow morning."

Borman agreed, hung up the phone and quietly told Susan and the boys what Slayton had just told him. They packed hurriedly and drove back to Houston; without even stopping at their own home, they pulled up across the street from the Whites' house, finding a space to park wherever they could among the astronaut sports cars and government sedans that were already crowding the curb. They went inside—no need to knock today, just as there was never a need to knock when an astronaut was in space and the family's home was filled with well-wishers around the clock, serving the cake and sandwiches and coffee during the day and the casserole and potato salad in the evenings. On those bright, busy days, everyone would be walking the wire between excitement and terror, a balancing act that would last until splashdown.

But tonight, terror had won. The feared thing had happened and the people in the room showed it: they were drawn and hollow-eyed, subdued and deeply sorrowful. Susan rushed to Pat, who was surrounded by the wives, and they embraced like sisters. Borman joined the astronaut cluster, exchanging grim nods and murmured condolences. The government people, in their own small group, spoke in the low and purposeful tones they used when working at something important. And what they were working on right now were the funerals. That, from what Borman could hear, was also what Pat was talking about with Susan—when she could work her words through her hitching breath.

The decision had already been made that all three astronauts would be buried at Arlington National Cemetery sometime next week, just as John Kennedy had been buried there a little more than three years before. It was precisely the kind of honor the men deserved, except that Ed White wanted nothing to do with Arlington, Kennedy or not. Like his father, White had been a West Point man, and more than once he had made it clear to Pat that since he had learned to be a soldier and taken his commission at the academy, he wanted to be buried there if he lost his life in the race for space. Washington, however, had decided there would be just one funeral for the entire crew; it was neater that way, especially since President Lyndon Johnson planned to attend.

Susan summoned Borman and told him of the problem. Pat pleaded with him to set things right. He nodded.

"Ed will be buried at West Point," he promised Pat.

"But they said there could be only one service," she responded.

"There will be two," he said.

Then he walked to the government men, asked for the phone number of whichever protocol office had dispatched them here and dialed it with a jabbing finger.

"This is Frank Borman," he said when the man answered. "I'm at Ed White's house. It is his family's wishes that he be buried at West Point."

The man began to protest, explaining that the Arlington arrangements were already being made.

"I don't care," Borman said. "Ed will be buried at West Point as the family wants. Now go make *those* arrangements, because that is what is going to happen."

He hung up the phone, leaving it rattling in its receiver. Borman would be at the Cape in the morning as ordered, but later in the week he would be traveling to West Point to help carry his friend to his grave.

✴ ✴ ✴ ✴ ✴ ✴ ✴ ✴

Not long after Borman arrived at the Cape, he visited the launch-pad and climbed inside the ruined *Apollo*. The spacecraft was still perched atop its rocket to nowhere and from a distance, in the right light, the bright white ghost ship still looked ready to fly someplace grand.

By now, the bodies had been removed and sent off to the medical examiner's office. Yet there wouldn't be much of an examination: it was already clear that the men had died not of burns, but of suffocation. The fire had flashed through too fast to have consumed much of the cloth of their suits, but the smoke and the fumes from a thousand melting materials would have been impossible to survive for long.

Grissom had been found partly in his left-hand couch and partly slumped under White's in the center, suggesting that when he died he was performing his part in the evacuation drill by leaning over to assist White as he tried to open the latches on the hatch. White died in his own couch doing that work, with one arm dropped across his face as if he were trying to protect himself from the poisonous smoke that had filled the ship. Chaffee, too, was still in his seat; his assignment would have been to maintain radio contact with the ground throughout the escape, the likely reason his voice was heard first.

By the time Borman climbed inside, a plastic drop cloth had been hung over the instrument panel and spread on the seats, keeping the death scene pristine until the plastic could be rolled back bit by bit during the mechanical autopsy to come. It would be an exceedingly painstaking job.

The deconstruction would go on for several months. Ultimately, the work would reveal the precise sequence of small, avoidable problems that had led to the tragedy on the launchpad.

At precisely 6:31 p.m. on the night of the fire, a spark had jumped from a wire on the far left of the spacecraft, beneath Gus Grissom's seat. The wire ran beneath a little storage compartment with a metal door that had been opened and closed many times without anybody noticing that each time the door moved, it wore away a little more of the wire's insulation, finally leaving the wire free to spark at will. When the wire sparked during the plugs-out test, it ignited a small fire that stayed small only for a second or two. Accelerated by the pure oxygen, the flames climbed along the left-hand wall of the spacecraft, feeding on fabric and netting used for storage. That wall was the worst possible place for a fire to erupt since it prevented Grissom from reaching a latch that would have opened a valve and vented the high-pressure atmosphere, thus slowing the flames.

Unimpeded, the fire proceeded to consume anything around it that would burn—the paper of the flight plans, the cloth of the seats, the Velcro and plastic and rubber that were everywhere. It fed on the space suits of the men themselves, spreading over Grissom and toward White, who by now was struggling with the hopeless ratchet and the locked-tight hatch. As the temperature climbed inside the ship, the pressure soared, causing a weak spot on the floor on the far right of the cabin to do what the person who shouted "Clear the level!" feared, which was to rupture.

The explosion ripped apart not only the doomed spacecraft, but all the plans NASA had so carefully drawn for its steady march to the moon. The astronauts would be mourned by the nation, the space agency would be condemned by the press and both houses of Congress would investigate the accident and issue scalding reports. To no one's surprise, NASA indefinitely suspended all planned flights of the *Apollo* spacecraft.

* * * * * * * *

Only when the deconstruction of the accident was complete did Borman move on to the real job he had in the investigation, which was to go out to Downey to work on the factory floor. Appointed by NASA administrator Jim Webb and Deke Slayton, Borman was the astronauts' chief representative and advocate, which kept him away from home for even longer stretches than usual. It was far too late in the game to sack North American Aviation and start over with a new contractor. Instead, the place would have to be reformed.

Wally Schirra was on-site, too, but in a sense, he wasn't there at all—not the real Wally at least. As the commander of *Apollo 1*'s backup crew, Schirra figured that he had a bigger stake than anyone else in making sure the spacecraft got fixed, which meant that the jolly Wally everyone knew was nowhere to be seen.

"You roasted three men in that thing already," he would snap at anyone on the floor at Downey who objected to inter-ference from an astronaut. "You're not going to roast me."

But through it all, the *Apollo* spacecraft was slowly being redesigned and rebuilt. The wiring was rewoven; the hatch was replaced with a new model that could be opened by one person in seconds; the flammable Velcro was eliminated. Every shred of ordinary paper was replaced by fireproof paper, and every scrap of ordinary cloth was replaced by fireproof beta cloth. Combustible coolant was replaced, soldered joints were reworked, vibrational tests were improved and the 100-percent-oxygen atmosphere used on the pad was replaced by a nitrogen-oxygen mix. Every single step in the quality control and checkout processes was also rethought and redrafted.

Most important, the engineers and the human-factors people at North American would never again be allowed to slip the leash of the space agency.

"Nobody's going to put anything in the spacecraft unless NASA management approves it," said Borman—who as far as North American was concerned *was* NASA management.

And nobody ever did.

SIX

1967–1968

NOBODY FULLY APPRECIATED what a bright, hopeful charm the moon had been until it was suddenly moved back out of reach. The steady climb to a lunar landing had been exciting and energizing, with the spaceships flying and the calendar cooperating, and for a while it seemed almost certain that NASA would meet the challenge President Kennedy had thrown down. Now there was nothing; the deadline was only three years away and the ships, for the moment at least, were grounded. And what remained was a national mess that stretched well beyond NASA.

If 1967 had been birthed in a fast, hot fire at the Cape, other, larger fires soon seemed to be breaking out everywhere else. Lyndon Johnson, who rose to the presidency after President Kennedy was assassinated, could point proudly to his Voting Rights Act and his Civil Rights Act to protect the right to vote and to ensure equal protection under the law no matter the color of one's skin, but laws counted for little if the people they were meant to benefit were still suffering in rural poverty in the South and in broken, stultifying ghettos in the North. That summer, as the nation endured a record-setting heat wave, more than 125 US cities erupted in race riots, and many of them were put to the torch. New York burned in late July when cars were overturned and set ablaze in the segregated neighborhood of Harlem. Newark's fires raged for four terrible days; riots killed twenty-three people and injured a thousand. Detroit followed, with forty-three deaths, 1,189 injuries and 7,200 arrests. Firefighters abandoned one hundred square blocks of the city, which quickly burned to the ground, the flames hurried along by twenty-five-mile-per-hour winds that struck at just the wrong time.

In October, fires of a different sort were lit, as more than one hundred thousand antiwar protesters, fed up with the endless combat in Southeast Asia, marched on Washington, rallying first at the Lincoln Memorial and then across the Potomac River at the Pentagon. Their loathing of Johnson and his Vietnam adventure was clear. The blood in which Johnson's presidency had begun seemed to be rising back up and threatening to drown him entirely.

Within NASA, the mood was equally bleak. Everyone understood that 1967 was going to be a washout, at least in terms of getting American astronauts off the launchpad. In an agency known for its bravado, doubt crept in. How could it not? The moon project depended on a spacecraft that had proven itself a literal death trap, a *Saturn V* rocket that had never carried men into orbit and a lunar excursion module that hadn't even been completely built. Nobody at NASA was more impatient to see the Apollo program start flying than the astronauts themselves,

Frank Borman among them. And after putting in his time on the factory floor at Downey, Borman was ready to get back into the air.

✳ ✳ ✳ ✳ ✳ ✳ ✳ ✳

No matter how eager the astronauts were to return to space, the *Saturn V* rocket first had to get off the ground—and that was going to take some doing.

Traveling from the launchpad in Florida to the plains of the moon was, at bottom, a business of using a very big rocket to get a very large spacecraft moving very, very fast—faster than human beings had ever traveled before. That called for a rocket unlike any that had ever been built, and NASA never tired of wowing the world with the size of the monster they had invented. The *Saturn V* stood 363 feet tall—or the height of a thirty-six-story building or sixty feet taller than the Statue of Liberty or forty feet longer than a football field, including the end zones.

The monster's weight was just as impressive. Fully fueled, a *Saturn V* tipped the scales at 6.5 million pounds, or a third again as heavy as a navy destroyer. But a navy destroyer moved on its belly, sliding across the surface of the ocean, a prisoner of gravity. The *Saturn V* flew.

As the rocket shot away from Earth, it would begin shedding stages as each burned through its fuel, and none of these stages took very long. The first stage took less than three minutes before it was done with its job. In that time, each of the giant rocket's five first-stage engines gulped three tons of kerosene and liquid oxygen fuel per second, burning through more than half a million gallons—the same as burning through the gas tanks of more than thirty thousand cars—in just 168 seconds. At an altitude of thirty-six miles, the first stage was jettisoned, allowing the second to take over. The second stage carried five smaller engines that burned through 885 gallons of fuel every second for six minutes. After that came a third stage with a single engine that would give the astronauts the final kick into Earth orbit and would later be lit a second time to sling them out toward the moon.

But this extraordinary machine was also extraordinarily dangerous. When the first stage was lit and the rocket was just beginning to haul itself off the pad, the engines would be generating 160 million horsepower—as much energy as would be produced if every river and stream in the United States were running through a single hydroelectric turbine at once. Only a nuclear explosion would produce a louder man-made sound than a *Saturn V* taking off. And if the rocket went rogue and exploded on takeoff, the blast would create a massive fireball that could melt steel.

The first launch of the monster machine—the mission called Apollo 4—took place on the morning of November 9, 1967. The show was sensational. Spectators crowded the Florida coast the way they usually would only for a crewed flight, and they got what they came for.

"My golly, our building's shaking here! Our building's shaking!" shouted Walter Cronkite in his temporary studio, three miles from the launch site. Inside the makeshift newsroom, the picture window facing the launchpad began rattling in its frame and the crew in the booth leapt forward to hold it in place.

"The roar is terrific!" he called, as the building's ominous-sounding tremors became audible to viewers. "This big glass window is shaking, we're holding it with our hands! Look at that rocket go! Part of our roof is coming in here!"

Things weren't much calmer in the firing room that was Cape Kennedy's Mission Control. Plaster dust rained down from the ceiling, settling on consoles that were typically kept free of the slightest bit of dirt. The engine's thunder produced vibrations that were detected as far north as New York. The controllers whooped and cheered at their dusty desks. Even Wernher von Braun, the rocket's head designer, who was using binoculars to watch the launch through the firing room's more robust window, allowed himself a moment of jubilation.

"Go, baby, go!" shouted the German designer, who had never been heard to call anyone or anything "baby" before.

It took less than twelve minutes for the third stage of the *Saturn* and the uncrewed *Apollo* spacecraft to reach Earth orbit, and once the rocket and its cargo got there, they did everything that was asked of them. The *Apollo* beamed down healthy vital signs to Houston, reassuring administrators that if astronauts had been aboard, they'd be just fine. After about three hours— or two orbits—into the flight, the third stage fired to boost the *Apollo* from its safe, 119-mile-high orbit to a nosebleed altitude of 11,000 miles, after which, the command module separated and flawlessly executed the acrobatic, deep-space reentry, landing less than ten miles from the prime splashdown site near Hawaii.

But if *Apollo 4* hit every mark, the next two missions weren't quite so flawless—and that's being charitable. *Apollo 5*, which was launched by a *Saturn 1B* rocket, was riddled with errors and *Apollo 6* was, in Chris Kraft's words, "a disaster," with the *Saturn V* rocket shaking violently as it flew. If astronauts had been aboard, they might have been killed by the so-called pogo problem.

Seventeen months had now elapsed since an American astronaut had flown in space, and the next flight on the docket, *Apollo 7*, was supposed to be a crewed flight, though it didn't seem like the space agency was remotely ready. Only twenty months remained before an American was supposed to set foot on the moon. For the moment, the country's space program seemed to be moving in reverse.

✳ ✳ ✳ ✳ ✳ ✳ ✳ ✳

If 1967 was a tragic year, 1968 was going to be a blood-soaked one. The Vietnam War was spiraling out of control with American and civilian casualties soaring. Riots at home prompted President Johnson not to seek reelection. To the shock and horror of the nation, the great civil rights leader Dr. Martin Luther King Jr. was assassinated. Just two months later, Senator Bobby Kennedy, the brother of the slain President John F. Kennedy, was assassinated, too.

Through it all—quietly, doggedly—the engineers and planners and astronauts at NASA labored on. In their windowless rooms, on their guarded bases, they lost track nearly altogether of the flaming world around them. To the extent that they noticed the explosions of violence at all, they were a dull thumping beyond the walls, a dim flashing through a very thick scrim. It was there, too, that George Low, Director of the Apollo Spacecraft Program Office, would give voice to a brainstorm that would change everything.

Exactly what Low said was remembered one way by Low himself and another by Chris Kraft and a third by Bob Gilruth, the head of the Manned Spaceflight program in Houston. But all three men were present the day the chief of the Apollo program asked his two colleagues to listen to what he had been thinking. And what Low said, in effect, was: *You know our schedule? Let's forget our schedule. Let's go to the moon in sixteen weeks. And let's give the job to Apollo 8.*

* * * * * * * *

George Low had a lot of reasons for taking his Mad Hatter chance and proposing an early flight to the moon. One big reason involved the Soviet Union. The death of the *Apollo 1* crew had shaken both countries' space programs badly. But even though the Soviets expressed sympathy for the loss of the *Apollo 1* crew, Moscow, where the Russian government made its plans, wasn't blind to an opportunity. A slowdown in the American program gave the Soviets a clear lane, at least for a while. And by the summer of 1968, they were making the most of it. Word pinging across America's own intelligence web had it that Russian space engineers had been aggressively testing their new crewed spacecraft, the *Zond*, with plans to launch the next two, *Zond 5* and *Zond 6*, on circumlunar flights, whipping around the moon and coming back home. It wouldn't be a lunar landing—it wouldn't even be a lunar orbit—but it would still be a first-ever trip to the moon and back, meaning that the first eyes ever to see the lunar farside would be Russian. Yes, for *Zond 5* at least, they would be mouse or bug or hamster eyes. But assuming the animal passengers survived the trip, Russian astronauts, known as cosmonauts, would follow, quite possibly before the end of the year.

That got Low's teeth gnashing and his thoughts churning, which in turn led to his brainstorm. He wanted to go to the moon on a circumlunar flight. He wanted *Apollo 8* to make the trip. He told Gilruth and Kraft that the lunar mission would be approved only if the Apollo 7 Earth orbital mission—the first crewed Apollo mission—was "very good, if not perfect." And he had a final requirement: if they went ahead with the moon trip, it had to happen before the end of the year, or in roughly four months. There was simply no more time to waste.

Hoping not to spook Gilruth and Kraft too much, Low had deliberately used the term "circumlunar" as opposed to the less specific "moon flight." A circumlunar flight, like the one the Russians were apparently planning, would keep the crew on what was known as a free-return trajectory, meaning that even if their Service Propulsion Engine—SPS, in the engineers' shorthand—failed them completely on the way out, lunar gravity would whip them around the far side of the moon and toss them home. Actually orbiting the moon, however, would require the SPS to work perfectly, not once, but twice: the first time to settle the ship into lunar orbit and the second to blast it out.

Gilruth was reasonably certain that Low couldn't be suggesting that brand of insanity. But just to be certain, he checked.

"What kind of mission?" he finally asked. "Just out and back? A circumlunar trip?"

"Yes, that's what I'm thinking," Low assured him quickly.

When Kraft at last found his voice, he couldn't say much that was terribly positive, even about such a straightforward trip to the moon. "I have to think about it awhile," he said. "I can't give you an answer. We had all the stuff laid out according to our game plan and that ruins our game plan." He shook his head. "We'll have to go back and look at everything."

That was exactly what Low expected Kraft to say, and he was reasonably confident that once Kraft did look at everything, he would realize that at least some of the pieces for the revised mission were already in place. The command-service module, or CSM, was more or less ready, which was no small accomplishment. The command portion, which was eleven feet tall and shaped like a cone, would house the astronauts; the service module, a cylindrical, twenty-four-foot structure that was attached to the rear of the command module like the trailer behind the cab of a truck, contained the spacecraft's main engine, the SPS, as well as much of its essential hardware, like oxygen tanks, water supply, batteries and fuel cells. The engine's bell extended another twelve feet behind the service module. At the very end of the mission, just as the astronauts were nearing

Earth, they would jettison the service module and descend through the atmosphere in the command module alone, which had a heat shield at the bottom to protect it.

The hard work that had been done since the fire had made it possible for NASA to certify the command-service module for flight. But that was only the hardware. What the computer guys called the "software"—the programming for the electronic brains both in the spacecraft and on the ground—had not yet been fully written.

The *Saturn V*, meanwhile, had lost the confidence of a lot of people and would somehow have to be proven flightworthy. And the Mission Controllers—the people who would actually be managing the flight and be in constant contact with the spacecraft—had not yet begun intensive rehearsals for a moon journey they all assumed was at least a year away.

Then there was the matter of training a crew, one that could be made ready to fly in so short a time. That not inconsiderable detail was on Gilruth's mind, too. "Deke needs to be a part of this conversation," he said, picking up his phone and dialing Slayton's phone number.

The chief astronaut arrived and sat. Low presented the plan he had just described to Gilruth and Kraft; betraying nothing, Slayton chewed on it for a moment. As an astronaut, he preferred ambitious risk-taking to methodical plan-making, but as the man charged with the safety of the astronauts who actually had flown and would fly some more, he had to be more cautious.

"I think I could train up a crew," he said. "That's not a

concern. But as to the idea itself . . ." He trailed off. "I need to think about this carefully for a couple of days."

Low nodded, and then he and Gilruth sent Kraft and Slayton off to begin working out the details. But just as they were standing to leave, Gilruth gestured for them to wait.

"Tell no one about this," he said, "no one except the people who absolutely must know. And whatever you do, say nothing to the press."

The two men agreed, and when they reached the hall, Kraft looked at Slayton. "You go do your thing," he said. "I'll go do mine."

✱ ✱ ✱ ✱ ✱ ✱ ✱ ✱

For Slayton, there wasn't much to do, nor was there anyone to consult—except himself. Whatever decision he reached would rest almost entirely on his granular knowledge of the training and the aptitudes of his Apollo crews. He would not reveal anything to the astronauts themselves, all of whom would surely campaign for the circumlunar plan. He alone would decide if there was a team of three ready to make the flight.

Slayton would spend a few days thinking it all through; his committee of one needed a bit more reflection before he made his announcement. But if he had to make the call today, he knew what it would be. *Apollo 8*'s Jim McDivitt, Dave Scott and Rusty Schweickart had already done a lot of training in their lunar module and it would be a shame to waste all of that work and send them on a mission with only a command-service module. *Apollo 9*'s Borman, Lovell and Anders had not done much LEM training yet at all. Plus, Borman and Lovell had worked together extremely well on *Gemini 7*, a mission no one else had wanted, and that kind of experience would help them on *Apollo 8*.

For Kraft, there could be no such solitary contemplation. He needed a real committee—a small, trusted group of deputies—who could work with him behind tightly closed doors.

The moment he returned to his office, he summoned a handful of colleagues, including two key lieutenants: Bill Tindall, the orbital mechanics expert who would effectively manage the physics of any lunar trip, and John Hodge, director of flight planning, who would write the mission script, a blow-by-blow detailed plan of every moment of the mission and the roles of every player on the ground and in the air. Kraft was reassured to see that none of them responded with wide eyes or a flat "no" to Low's proposal. Indeed, all of them seemed pleased, even excited, by the idea.

Kraft's group began talking it through, especially the question of the timeline, which would require them not just to do something they had never done before, but to do it in a sprint. Yet the more they talked, the more they realized that although there were many obstacles, none of them seemed insurmountable. Kraft, satisfied with what he was hearing, sent the team out to discuss it further—*among themselves only,* he reminded them—and told them to return tomorrow with an answer that was a product of more detailed reflection and a decent night's sleep.

When Kraft's deputies trooped back into his office the

next day, the answer they provided was not at all what he had anticipated.

"We think it's a great idea," Tindall said. "We don't know whether we can do it or not, but it's worth a try." Kraft nodded, but Tindall wasn't through. "There's one thing we want to do, which you haven't mentioned, and you're probably going to be upset about. We don't just want to go to the moon. We want to go into orbit around the moon."

Now Kraft was truly at a loss. Looking around the circle of engineers, he immediately fulfilled his most important responsibility, which was to ask the critical question: "Why would you want to increase the risk?"

His men were ready with an answer. For starters, flying to the moon was a huge commitment of resources and training, and flying there just to whip around once, take a peek at the lunar farside and then return home seemed like a terrible waste. Yes, going into lunar orbit would mean that the SPS would have to work perfectly, but the engine would have to do that on any trip to the moon, and it would get a thorough shakedown on *Apollo 7* first. If you couldn't trust the machine to do its job, you never should have built it in the first place.

If the administrators were uneasy about the reliability of the SPS, it was partly because they had been thinking too hard to the media. There were 5.6 million separate parts in the command-service module, the agency would say, which meant that even if everything worked 99.9 percent perfectly, 5,600 parts might go wrong. That shocking number was intended mostly to wow the public with the exacting nature of the work the space agency was doing, but NASA's engineers knew the statistic was meaningless, since you would never send men into space in a machine with a performance rating of 99.9 percent. Three or four nines on the right-hand side of that decimal point were the minimum threshold for good design. Just as important, one of the reasons that the command-service module had millions of parts was that many of those parts were redundant, backups or even backups to backups, and they would never be used unless the part they were supporting failed.

If the engine was reliable enough for a lunar-orbit mission, and Kraft's engineers believed it was, there was another excellent reason not to limit the mission to a circumlunar one. America's uncrewed lunar spacecraft—its crash-landers and soft-landers and orbiters—had long been flummoxed by lunar gravity. The moon's gravitational field had bumps in it, unpredictable areas of more than the usual one-sixth g, and these bumps could potentially send a ship off course. The irregularities were the result of what the geologists called mascons (for mass concentrations), the remains of heavy-metal meteorites that had long ago crashed into the moon and buried themselves there. The mascons had been entirely harmless for billions of years, but as soon as a machine from Earth appeared, they would reach up with their invisible gravitational hands and shake the spacecraft in who-knew-what ways.

"Every time we plan trajectories with the gravitational models of the moon we have, we miss by two miles," Tindall told Kraft. "But if we could put the command module in orbit, we could develop an empirical set of formulas that would help us do the right orbit prediction." Ten orbits seemed like a sensible number of circuits to make around the moon. That would allow for the collection of a good mascon data set, not to mention photographs of the surface that would be used to plan later landings.

This argument, Tindall knew, would carry a lot of weight with his boss. Though a lunar-orbit mission meant increasing the risk for *Apollo 8*, it also meant decreasing it for every lunar *Apollo* that would follow. It was simple arithmetic, and Kraft loved arithmetic.

After talking it through for a bit longer, Kraft dismissed Tindall and the rest of his team to go run more numbers to prove they could accomplish their part of the difficult planning. That would take a couple more days, which Kraft believed he and everyone else needed.

Finally, at the end of the week, he summoned the one other person whose opinion he most needed: Gene Kranz. Kranz had become such a critical figure in the overall operation of Mission Control that he no longer had the time to man a console on every mission. Instead, he was working every other flight, serving as flight director only on odd-numbered missions; as a consequence, he wouldn't be chained to a control-room chair for *Apollo 8*. This was the best possible news for Kraft, since he needed Kranz to take a more sweeping hand in planning for the mission and determining whether it could be flown at all.

When Kranz arrived, Kraft got straight to business. He wanted to know if the computers were up to the task of sending three men to the moon in December.

Kranz borrowed Kraft's phone and called Bob Ernal, his

chief computer man. Ernal ran all the computers in Building 12 and Building 30 for a whole weekend to figure it out, and on Monday reported back to his higher-ups. Yes, he said, it could be done. If all the other parts of the operation were in place for a launch, his computers would put *Apollo 8* into orbit around the moon—and, more important, they would get the ship home again.

✳ ✳ ✳ ✳ ✳ ✳ ✳ ✳

Bit by bit, system by system, the levers of the great American moon machine were being thrown, and the gears were meshing and beginning to turn. But there was one final part to address, the biggest, loudest, most powerful one of all: the *Saturn V*. If there were no rocket, there could be no moon trip.

No sooner had the good word came back from Ernal, than Gilruth met with Low and Kraft once more, and told them, "Before we commit to this, we're going to have to get Wernher on board." He picked up his phone and called Wernher von Braun's office at the Marshall Space Flight Center in Huntsville, Alabama, where the *Saturn V* was designed and parts of it were built.

The chief designer's secretary answered. "He's in a meeting," she said. "Can he call you back?"

"No," Gilruth said. "He needs to come to the phone now."

The surprised secretary went off to collect von Braun. When he picked up the receiver and said hello, Gilruth told him that he, Low and Kraft needed to come talk to him.

"I can probably see you tomorrow," von Braun said.

"No, I want to see you right now."

"What do you mean?"

"We'll fly over there right now and talk to you," Gilruth answered, concluding the call before von Braun could object.

Kraft looked at Gilruth and could not completely contain a smile. He was, he knew, in a cowboy business, and he tried never to let the thrill of the work color his decisions. But today he simply couldn't help it. He phoned the commissary for sandwiches, grabbed them to go and then he, Gilruth and Low hopped aboard the Gulfstream plane they used to fly from Houston to Huntsville or Cape Kennedy.

When the three men got to Huntsville, they went straight to von Braun's office. They shared their new plan for *Apollo 8* and asked him if his rocket could be ready in time. Von Braun's face told them his answer. The idea of going to the moon before the end of the year was irresistible. His first *Saturn V* had flown brilliantly; his second had mostly botched the job. His third would make no such mistakes.

"Yes," the chief designer told his visitors. "Yes, we can be ready in time."

Then came the final hurdle—three hurdles, actually, and none of them had anything to do with machinery. All the moon talk would come to nothing if the plans for *Apollo 8* didn't get the approval of Jim Webb, the NASA administrator, and George Mueller, his deputy for crewed spaceflight, who were attending a conference in Vienna, and, of course, President Lyndon Johnson.

"Can't do that!" Mueller snapped when Low reached him and Webb on the phone overseas. "That's craziness!"

Webb was even angrier. "You try to change the entire

direction of the program while I'm out of the country?" he asked, incredulous. But he agreed not to rule it out until he returned home in a few days. That would be on August 22, and when he arrived, he wanted to meet with the entire team of lunar plotters.

The day arrived and Webb and Mueller came to Houston willing—but remotely not expecting—to be persuaded by the pitch they were about to hear. In the meeting that followed, the same scene that had unfolded over and over in Houston during the preceding weeks was repeated: one or two deeply skeptical men listened quietly and carefully, and then slowly became swept up in the ambition and vision and sheer power of the plan they were hearing. And just like the people in those earlier meetings, they came away agreeing that it was time—and there was reason—to take a very big risk.

Webb reasoned that he was bound by a promise he had made to himself in November of 1963, after the president who had hired him to run the nation's space program had been slain: he had pledged that he would get the US to the moon before 1970, even if it meant throwing the dice now and then.

Yes, Webb agreed, he would take this plan to President Johnson, along with his recommendation that the president approve it. He had no doubt that Johnson, with his deep feeling for the space program, would quickly agree. And he was right.

SEVEN

Summer and Fall 1968

THE PHONE CALL that came for Frank Borman, Jim Lovell and Bill Anders at the North American Aviation plant in Downey, California, was an unwelcome disruption. They had less than nine months to get ready for their *Apollo 9* launch, they hadn't had nearly enough practice time inside their command module and Anders, an eager rookie from the third astronaut class, had barely gotten his hands on his lunar excursion module, or LEM, the spidery lunar lander that would one day touch the surface of the moon and which was to be his primary responsibility for the mission. Borman didn't know Anders terribly well, but the newcomer already had a reputation as a lunar module wizard who made it his business to understand the strange machine better even than the men who had designed it.

Still, when the technician who came to fetch Borman told him that Slayton was on the line, the call could not be refused. Borman muttered a "carry on" to Lovell and Anders and hurried off. Not until the next day, when he returned to Downey, did he tell his crewmates what Slayton had told him.

"We're flying early, in December," he reported, dropping

the smaller news first. Lovell and Anders looked mildly surprised. "And we're going to orbit the moon."

Surprise turned to something approaching shock, but both astronauts were clearly delighted.

"Tight, but we can do it," Lovell said, and Borman nodded agreement.

"But the LEM's not ready," Anders pointed out.

This was the part Borman had dreaded. "No LEM," he said. "Just the CSM."

Anders's face fell. The moon was fine, wonderful actually, but losing his LEM was like losing a limb. A man could be on a command module track or a lunar module track. He had been the frontrunner on the LEM track, but now someone else would take his place, someone who would spend the next sixteen weeks continuing to train to fly the lander while Anders switched his attention to the less complex, less fanciful command module.

Still, there was no denying that serving as a crew member on the first trip to the moon would be truly historic. And part of Anders's new assignment, as Borman now explained it to him, would be to manage photographic and eyeball surveillance on possible lunar landing sites, a job that would take advantage of Anders's specialty in geology. This would be a critical part of the mission, since nobody could yet say with certainty whether the smooth plains—the so-called seas—on the surface of the moon that were being targeted for future missions were the pristine landing sites they appeared to be or whether boulder fields or other irregularities would menace an LEM as it made its final approach on a future mission to the moon. What's more, flying so early in the lunar-mission cycle might well give him a chance at another flight, this time in the commander's seat. On balance, he guessed that what Borman had told him today was good, if not ideal, news.

Anders would still have to break the surprising news to his family. Borman mentioned that he had told Susan and the boys about the new plan already, when he was back in Houston, and that they had given their approval without hesitation or even much excitement. Anders expected he would get a similar reaction out of his brood.

He and his wife, Valerie, had five children—four boys and one girl, ages four through eleven. An aviator's wife before she was even old enough to vote, Valerie had long since grown accustomed to accepting her husband's flying assignments with calm, and a mission to the moon would be no exception. The children were equally unmoved. Growing up on an astronauts' block and going to a school with other astronauts' children, even the youngest ones knew little else but the life of an astronaut's child.

Most of the astronauts had been test pilots, so kids were used to the idea that their dads had a dangerous job and that they'd be away a lot. Once a family graduated to astronaut status, though, there were the occasional nuisances, like reporters scrambling to capture every move you made, even if you were just going to school or horsing around on the lawn. Kids devised all sorts of strategies to avoid the shutterbugs. Teenage Barbara Lovell once even made her getaway by sneaking over to her neighbor's garage, and laying down in the back seat of her friend's car to avoid the clicking cameras.

There were some perks, too, like private flights to special places and the free stuff American companies would shower on the First Families of spaceflight. Whenever there was a launch, the neighborhood transformed into a kind of traveling circus for the kids, a procession from house to house for the extended parties at the home of whoever was heading into space that day. The undercurrent of terror that may have preoccupied the adults in the room didn't quite reach the kids, certainly not the littlest ones. For them, the trays of cookies and platters of cakes with neighborhood friends were just another good time.

Only Lovell got much of a reaction from his family when he told them he was going to the moon. He and his wife, Marilyn, had been planning to take their two boys and two girls—who were now fifteen, thirteen, ten and two—to Mexico for the Christmas holidays, and Marilyn had already begun shopping for clothes and beach supplies for the trip. But NASA had now filled in the Lovells' holiday calendar for them.

"You know that Mexico trip we're planning?" Lovell asked Marilyn when he came home from California.

"I do," she said warily.

"Well, I'm thinking of going somewhere else instead."

"And where would that be?" Marilyn asked.

"The moon," he answered.

Marilyn, despite herself, smiled.

✹ ✹ ✹ ✹ ✹ ✹ ✹ ✹

Once NASA decided to go forward with a journey to the moon before the year was even out, the *Apollo 8* astronauts, Mission Controllers and flight planners had to move fast, especially Wernher von Braun's team. Immediately following the disastrous flight of *Apollo 6*, von Braun had gathered his entire Huntsville team to fix the problems in the *Saturn V* rocket that had almost wrecked the ship. Just to make sure he had all the smartest heads together in the same room, he had also summoned—either in person or by phone—nearly one thousand other engineers from every contractor, subcontractor and sub-subcontractor who might have a useful thought about how best to sort out the giant machine's multiple defects.

The pogo problem, where the rocket shakes and bounces like a pogo stick as it flies, the most critical issue, was traced to a simple fact that is true of all rockets: they burn fuel, and as that fuel vanishes, it leaves nothing behind. The lower the level of kerosene, liquid hydrogen and liquid oxygen in the tanks, the less mass there is to absorb the rocket's vibrations, which in turn leads to pogo swings.

The answer was to keep that emptying space full—but with what? The *Saturn V* engines had only one speed, which was full speed, and the only way for the rocket to accelerate continually as it climbed was for it to get lighter and lighter as its fuel burned away. That's how you get from zero miles per hour to the nearly 25,000 miles per hour it takes to get to the moon. The problem is, if you add something to the tank to fill the empty spaces, you will be adding weight, too.

The engineers solved the puzzle neatly with helium. It was

inert, so it wouldn't react with other chemicals in the tank, and it was light. All you had to do was steadily pump helium into the tops of the tanks to take the place of the fuel as it burned away, and the gas would absorb the launch swings like a properly inflated tire cushioning the bumps in a road.

These and other fixes and refinements gave von Braun the confidence that the next *Saturn V* would be fit to carry crew. And this made him confident that the *Apollo 8* crew could go to the moon.

But NASA itself wouldn't be convinced until more and more testing was complete. And this sped-up game plan called for scheduling the last test just three days before *Apollo 8*'s planned launch.

✦ ✦ ✦ ✦ ✦ ✦ ✦ ✦

Creating the necessary software and writing the needed computer code were other hurdles for to the *Apollo 8* team. Bob Ernal may have run every computer in Buildings 12 and 30 for an entire weekend, but a thumbs-up from Ernal after just two days of work was hardly the final answer. It was, in fact, only the signal that it was time for a lot more people to get together and do a lot more work. For this, the demanding and blunt Bill Tindall, who had played a central part in the debate within Chris Kraft's team about whether *Apollo 8* should orbit the moon, would again play a role.

Now, as the sixteen-week clock began to tick, Tindall took to spending more and more of his time at the Massachusetts

Institute of Technology (MIT) in Cambridge, Massachusetts, where the mission's software was being written and tested. Before long, four hundred engineers were working for Tindall.

The focus of most of their work was on the COLOSSUS software, the system that—after winning a years-long competition with other programs—was chosen as the one that would be used to navigate to and from the moon. But COLOSSUS wasn't completely ready, and while the pace of the work to make it fit for flight had already been fierce, now it would have to move at a full sprint.

The most serious concern was what to do in the event of software crashes, which occurred quite often and might never be entirely eliminated from the program. The key to responding to crashes was how quickly and seamlessly the system could reboot. On a three-day outward coast to the moon, you might be able to tolerate it if your computer went offline for a little while, but in the critical minutes or seconds before the engine burn that would cause the spacecraft to enter lunar orbit, a software crash would be absolutely unacceptable.

The work at MIT was focused on ensuring that the restarts following a crash would be fast and automatic. The computer's core operating program would have to know which systems to start up in which sequence, how to check the soundness of the systems as they came online and how to suspend all other non-essential operations aboard the spacecraft while that work was being done.

As the fall wore on, the bugs got written out of the software. When COLOSSUS was finally considered ready for flight, nobody could say with certainty if that confidence was well placed. But Tindall pronounced himself happy, and that counted for a lot.

* * * * * * * *

Assuming the *Apollo 8* spacecraft did get off the ground and did make it to the moon and did get back to Earth safely, there was still the business of rescuing the astronauts after splash-down. Technically, it wasn't a difficult problem: you sent out ships and plucked the crew out of the water, and in the seven years Americans had been flying in space, NASA and the navy had gotten very good at that job. But it was a massive logistical headache.

There were a few possible launch windows at the end of 1968, and all of them were dictated by the relative positions of the Earth and the moon. The moon was a moving target, orbiting the Earth at a speed of 2,288 miles per hour, meaning that when *Apollo 8* left the ground, it would not be aimed at the spot the moon was occupying in the sky at the moment, but where it would be three days hence—much the way hunters aim their buckshot ahead of a flock of flying ducks, rather than at the ducks themselves.

For *Apollo 8* to succeed, three conditions would have to be met: First, Earth would have to be at the precise spot in its rotation where the *Saturn V* could leave the ground, enter Earth orbit and then blast out to the moon at the proper angle of approach. Second, either the Atlantic or Pacific Ocean had to rotate into position so that it was underneath the spacecraft when, six days after launch, it arced through the atmosphere for splashdown. Third, the moon had to be in the right spot in its waxing and waning phases so that the portions of the surface the crew planned to survey as future landing sites would be illuminated by the sun. After much calculation, NASA determined that the best of the possible windows put the liftoff at 7:51 a.m. Eastern Standard Time on December 21, with the spacecraft going into lunar orbit on Christmas Eve and splashing down in the Pacific Ocean southwest of Hawaii in the predawn hours of December 27.

The location and timing of *Apollo 8*'s splashdown required that a complex set of orders be given to the recovery ships, and arranging for that wouldn't be easy. The navy was planning to give its sailors a short Christmas vacation, and the decision to keep some of them working so that they could recover the spacecraft would rest with Admiral John McCain, Jr., the commander of the Pacific Fleet and of all naval forces in Vietnam. McCain had a lot of skin in the Vietnam mess; his son, Naval Aviator John McCain III, was being held as a prisoner of war in North Vietnam, having been shot down and captured almost a year earlier. Still, the navy and its senior officers had a lot of responsibilities, and they included supporting the nation's space program—as long as that support didn't compromise naval operations.

It was Chris Kraft's job to persuade Admiral McCain that *Apollo 8* met these criteria. In October, Kraft flew out to Hawaii and addressed an auditorium full of navy officials, though most of his attention was directed at McCain, who sat smoking a large cigar, surrounded by his officers.

"Admiral," Kraft concluded after he gave a presentation about how he wanted to get American astronauts to the moon before the Russians could beat them to it, "I realize that the navy has made its Christmas plans and I'm asking you to change them. I'm here to request that the navy support us and have ships out there before we launch and through Christmas. We need you."

McCain did not need to give the request more than a moment's reflection. "Best darn briefing I've ever had," he said. "Give this young man anything he wants."

✳ ✳ ✳ ✳ ✳ ✳ ✳ ✳

If the teams in Huntsville and Cambridge and NASA head-quarters were sprinting toward December, the men in Houston were working even harder—specifically the three who would fly the *Apollo 8* spacecraft and the dozens who would rotate through the consoles at Mission Control. And if the engineers at MIT had their Tindall to run them ragged, the people in Houston had their simsups, and they were worse. The simsups were the simulation supervisors, the men whose job it was to make the work lives of others at NASA utterly miserable. You could actually see the simsups at work; they sat at their own bank of consoles on the right side of the Mission Control auditorium. But you couldn't quite get to them: a wall of glass separated them from the rest of the room, which was probably just as well.

For both astronauts and Mission Controllers, the bulk of

training involved running simulated missions, then running them again and again and again, so that everyone knew every step in every possible flight plan deeply, exhaustively, reflexively. And then the simsups would blow everything up. They would allow a routine rehearsal in Mission Control to run for a while, and then, with no warning, they would shut down three of the imaginary first-stage *Saturn V* engines when the rocket was only 1,000 feet off the launchpad. Or they would kill the communications systems five minutes after the crew had left Earth orbit on their way to the moon, and when controllers would try to switch to the backup system, they would take that out, too. Or they would crash the spacecraft's environmental system, which controlled the air and temperature in the spacecraft astronauts needed to survive, and then order the man at the environmental control console to get the system configured again before the astronauts died from lack of warmth or oxygen.

The astronauts rehearsed in a spacecraft simulator elsewhere on the Houston campus, and the simsups were just as merciless when working with them. They would get the crew all the way to the far side of the moon, overburn their main engine and then give them precisely three minutes to sort out the problem before their orbit irreversibly decayed and they headed for a crash landing on the lunar surface. They would send the command module into a high-speed spin halfway to the moon and then kill the thruster controls, meaning the crew would have to bring their backup systems online before they could even begin to stabilize their spacecraft—and they would have to do it all before the simulated spin rate got too high, at which point astronauts in a spacecraft that was actually spinning would suffer vertigo and lose consciousness.

Sometimes the simulations were run only with the astronauts or only with the Mission Controllers. Other times the simsups would conduct so-called integrated sims, when the people on both ends would play the same roles they'd play days or weeks later when the mission actually flew. That was the way astronauts and Mission Controllers had trained for every flight that had ever flown, and that was the way they trained for *Apollo 8*. Except this time they were training to fly to the moon—or, more accurately, they were *learning* to fly to the moon, since no one had ever done it before.

✶ ✶ ✶ ✶ ✶ ✶ ✶ ✶

Throughout the run-up to the launch of *Apollo 8*, it had remained a rock-solid condition that *Apollo 7*'s mission should, in George Low's words, be "very good, if not perfect," or the *Apollo 8* crew would not be going to the moon. When the time came for the Apollo 7 mission, everything went according to plan. Well, almost everything. The crew suffered from bad head colds while in flight, and exhibited even worse attitudes, arguing with ground controllers and sometimes simply refusing orders.

Still, it was all but universally agreed within NASA that the Apollo 7 mission turned out to be every bit the success Low had demanded: the command-service module had worked almost perfectly for the entire eleven days the crew was aloft. Especially important were the tests of the main engine, which repeatedly lit and shut down precisely on command. If *Apollo 7*'s engine performed so well in orbit around the Earth, there was no reason to think *Apollo 8*'s wouldn't do the same in orbit around the moon.

The lunar mission was on. Borman, Lovell and Anders were going to the moon.

* * * * * * * *

Nobody at the Central Research Institute building outside of Moscow, where the brain trust of the Soviet space program spent their days, could spare much of a thought for any space mission the Americans might or might not be planning. They had more important matters to mind at home.

In September, more or less as planned, they had launched their *Zond 5* spacecraft and whipped it around the moon with a cargo of turtles and worms and insects, bringing them within 1,200 miles of the lunar farside. The spacecraft returned to Earth, but its aim was poor and it missed the precise atmospheric corridor needed for the high-speed reentry. It didn't miss by much, however, and although the ride was rough and the spacecraft landed in the Indian Ocean, rather than in the steppes of Kazakhstan, the animals survived.

Making the mostly successful mission sweeter, the American surveillance ship USS *McMorris* happened to be loitering nearby when the *Zond* was recovered. The nest of spies aboard the ship would surely report back to Washington that the Soviet Union was about to beat them in space once more, this time with the first crewed mission to the moon.

But before attempting to achieve that milestone, the Soviets would need to launch at least one more uncrewed *Zond* flight, just to make sure a cosmonaut could survive the ride the turtles and worms and insects had. The Russian space engineers were sure they had solved the reentry problems; to prove the point, this time they would not only fly their animal passengers around the moon and back, they would land them a precise 9.9 miles from the launchpad. A cosmonaut who touched down that close to the pad would practically be within walking distance of the launch-site barracks.

Zond 6 launched on November 10. Like *Zond 5*, it swung around the far side of the moon and flew straight back to Earth. Then, as it entered the atmosphere, it became clear that this time it would actually do much better than its earlier *Zond* brother. The ship performed the reentry maneuver almost flawlessly. It plunged through the atmosphere, building up no more heat and no more g's than a human passenger could easily handle, and headed straight for a landing at the exact spot that had been planned.

The *Zond*'s parachute deployed when it was supposed to and its speed of descent slowed as it was supposed to. Then, just 3.3 miles above the ground—after a journey of some 230,000 miles—the ship did something it was absolutely not supposed to do until it had touched the Kazakh soil: it jettisoned its parachute due to an internal malfunction. There was nothing to save it then, nor would there have been a way to save a cosmonaut if one had been on board. After falling to the ground like the dead, multiton weight it was, the *Zond* half buried itself in the soil.

In the Central Research Institute building the next day, Nikolai Pilyugin, the chief designer of the *Zond*'s guidance system, gathered his engineers for a dressing-down. "Finally," Pilyugin shouted, "all the systems activated without a problem and you managed to shoot off the parachute when it was almost on the ground! And you were dreaming that we were about to launch a human being?"

Even if Americans didn't know it yet, the Soviets were now very unlikely to beat them in the race to the moon.

EIGHT

Christmas Week 1968

IF THERE WAS a great big party taking place in Florida on the weekend of December 20, 1968—and there was—the *Apollo 8* astronauts weren't invited to it. Nobody counted the precise number of people pouring out of the cars that were swarming toward Cape Kennedy and parking along its beach roads and in its motel lots, but the best guess put it at about a quarter of a million. Likewise, no one could say how far all these people had traveled to get here, but the license plates came from dozens of states as well as Canada—far more than just Florida's Deep South neighbors, whose residents could usually be counted on to show up no matter how routine the launch.

Borman, Lovell and Anders saw little of the crowd or the VIPs or the reporters who swarmed the Cape, and they liked that just fine, especially Borman. The hullabaloo surrounding the mission was a distraction, and not one he welcomed. Borman had tolerated a recent White House dinner celebrating the astronauts—he was mainly glad that Susan had enjoyed it. She and Valerie Anders would be going home to Houston to watch the launch on TV, while Marilyn Lovell and the four Lovell children would go to the Cape. If Susan had to say good-bye to Frank Borman, doing so on the morning after being toasted by the President of the United States seemed fair and fitting given the risks that he—and, by extension, the Borman family at large—was taking.

But once the White House business was done, Borman found the plain and simple crew quarters on the Cape Kennedy grounds something of a relief. The ten days at the Cape before the launch would be spent shuttling between there and the *Apollo* simulators, with intermittent briefings by the trajectory experts and flight planners. Still, even in semi-isolation, the crew would suffer the occasional intrusions, which generally came from the odd celebrity who asked NASA for an audience with the astronauts and then was persistent enough to ask more than once.

One important and complicated VIP tour was the visit by the flying legend Charles Lindbergh, who made the first trans-atlantic flight, traveling from New York to Paris. Lindbergh had shadowed the astronauts down to the Cape, but he didn't come knocking until the day before the launch. Borman, for one, didn't know quite what to make of him. Both he and Lovell were born in 1928, just one year after Lindbergh's famous flight, and they grew up adoring the great aviator. In recent years, though, most Americans—including Borman and Lovell—lost respect for Lindbergh. Before World War II, he showed himself to be a Nazi sympathizer, spouting hateful propaganda and arguing against American involvement in the coming war.

Now, three decades later, the once-great aviator was tapping on the door of the crew quarters and asking for a few minutes of the crew's time. The *Apollo 8* astronauts let him in around lunchtime on December 20. They all sat down together and ate, after which the dishes were supposed to be cleared and the visitor was supposed to leave.

Instead, the four men continued talking. Or, more accurately, Lindbergh talked—about the early age of flying, about the aviators he'd known, about the fifty combat missions he'd flown for the US in the Pacific theater, having decided to help the United States fight World War II.

The astronauts listened long and attentively. As the afternoon wore on, they at last began to speak about their own mission, which, as a glance at the clock and the lengthening shadows told them, would get under way in less than sixteen hours. At first they spoke almost reluctantly, because if a flight to the moon would be a rather more ambitious affair than a flight across the Atlantic, Lindbergh had already achieved his great deed, while Borman, Lovell and Anders had yet to do theirs. Lindbergh was attentive as they spoke and asked them a few questions about their spacecraft and their rocket. As they answered, he picked up a piece of notepaper that was sitting on the table and began to scribble something on it, glancing up once or twice to show he was listening. Finally, he stopped and looked at the three men.

"In the first second of your mission tomorrow," he said, "you will use ten times more fuel than I used on my entire flight." With that, the tarnished old flier showed his respect, making it clear that he would accept no more diffidence from the three young men who were about to make their own historic marks as pilots.

✳ ✳ ✳ ✳ ✳ ✳ ✳ ✳

Borman and Anders would have a bit of time to reflect on the singular experience of having spent an afternoon with the likes of Charles Lindbergh, but Lovell would have no such luxury. While his crewmates had only the mission on their minds, Lovell had his entire family to attend to because Marilyn and their four children had taken up residence in a beach house not far from the launchpad.

Darkness came early on December 20, the shortest day of 1968. At about 5:30 p.m., Lovell drove over to the beach house, where he and Marilyn bundled the kids into the car. They drove in silence and the children chattered in the back seat while they wheeled onto Highway A1A toward the space center. After approaching the heavily guarded gate, Lovell flashed his Cape credentials, but the guard did not need to see them, beaming warmly at the lunar astronaut and his family.

More than three miles away, on a spit of land behind the space-center fortifications, stood the brilliant spike of white that was the *Saturn V.* Floodlit, the rocket was impossible to miss across the flat terrain. Lovell drove through the gate and past the space center's multiple buildings and blockhouses; as he drew closer to the launchpad, the thirty-six-story missile seemed to grow and grow.

The technicians crowding around the pad waved but gave the Lovell family room as they got out of the car on a nearby sand dune and gazed up, little Jeffrey in Marilyn's arms and the rest of the children standing nearby. NASA staff had set up a table on the sand and offered doughnuts and coffee. The Lovells were far too taken with the spectacle of the rocket to think about eating; the technicians, who were used to the sight of a *Saturn*, were happy for the distraction of a snack. Marilyn had seen the far smaller, steel-gray *Titan* boosters that had twice before taken her husband to space, but this was different. She craned her neck upward at the *Saturn V*; if some might find the rocket to be monstrous at such close remove, she had a single, surprising thought:

It's a work of art.

It wasn't a monster at all. It was gorgeous.

Marilyn and her children would watch it fly from a safe distance of three miles tomorrow morning, and it would take their dad to a very unsafe distance of nearly a quarter million miles. But at that moment, Marilyn could feel nothing but excitement for her husband and a deep awe at the machine.

"You know the roar is going to be something terrible," Lovell said as he stepped close to her and followed her gaze.

"We'll be all right," Marilyn assured him. "We saw the *Titan*s go."

"They were nothing like this," Lovell said.

Marilyn nodded.

"And don't worry when it leans," he added.

"Leans?" Marilyn asked.

Lovell nodded. "Just a degree or two to the right at liftoff so it doesn't hit the tower."

Marilyn tried to picture the massive object tilting even an inch off its perfectly upright line and then shook off the picture. If that was the way the thing needed to fly, that was how it would fly.

After a few more minutes, with the children getting restless, Marilyn took them back into the car and the family drove off the grounds and back to the beach house. Lovell joined them inside for a last good-bye and now, Marilyn noticed, he was carrying a manila envelope with him. He opened it up and produced a picture of the moon—a close-up of a wide, gray plain, taken by one of NASA's lunar orbiters.

"It's the Sea of Tranquility," he told her. Then he pointed to a small triangular mountain on the dry bank of the waterless sea. "This is one of the 'initial points' we'll be surveying. It's a landmark that a later crew will use when they begin their descent." Marilyn nodded, not certain why he was sharing this bit of mission detail. "I'll be one of the first people ever to see it," he said, "so I'm going to name it Mount Marilyn."

Marilyn's eyes filled with tears. Not trusting her voice, she simply gave him a hug and kissed him good-bye.

✳ ✳ ✳ ✳ ✳ ✳ ✳ ✳

Lovell returned to the astronaut quarters not long after 8:00 p.m., and once he did, the *Apollo 8* crew's flight to the moon effectively began. The astronauts were still on the ground, still in civilian clothes, still breathing the same air and walking the same ground as the other 3.6 billion people on the planet. But their departure clock had begun to run, and it was ticking insistently.

Liftoff would be the next morning at 7:51 a.m. Eastern Standard Time. That meant an old man's dinner hour of 5:30 p.m. Lovell had eaten before he went to the beach house; by the time he returned, Borman and Anders were getting ready for bed, and now he did the same. Wake-up, according to NASA's compulsively precise schedule, would come at 2:36 a.m.; a final medical check would follow at 2:51; breakfast would be at 3:21; suit-up would start at 3:56. At 4:42, the crew would walk out to the van that would take them to the launchpad. At 5:03, they would get to the pad, and by 5:11 they would have ridden the gantry elevator to the top and climbed into their spacecraft.

That was how the crew's prelaunch sequence was scripted, and when the planned moments arrived, that was exactly how it played out. The wake-up came the way it always did, with Deke Slayton letting himself into the astronauts' darkened suite and flipping the lights on in the common room. He then went from bedroom to bedroom, knocking on each door, opening it up so that the light could flood in, pointing at his watch and reminding the crew of what time it was and that breakfast call was in fifteen minutes: a menu of steak, eggs, toast, fruit, juice and coffee that was the same as it had been since the Mercury days.

The reporters massing outside in the predawn chill would not see the astronauts until they were suited up and ready to make the walk to the van. But there was a photographer present at the breakfast and he would follow the crew to the suit-up. Though the astronauts didn't mind the cameraman watching them eat, the suit-up photos were another matter.

A man being dressed for space was a lot less like a knight being dressed for battle than the public would want to know. Every stitch of the suit—with built-in temperature control, access to oxygen, and communications systems with Houston and their fellow astronauts—was critical to keeping the men alive in space, but that didn't make getting it on very easy. It was a slow and cumbersome process: each piece of space suit the astronaut donned left him more helpless and thus more dependent on the technicians to put on his boots and hoist up his pants and snap the wrist rings of his gloves into place on his sleeves. The result was a puffy, clumsy parade float of a man who, in a final indignity, would be required to spend the next several minutes lying down on a large recliner—a turtle on his back—prebreathing the canned air in his life-support systems to make sure he adjusted properly. Only then would he be helped back to his feet for the walk out to the van that would take him to the pad.

As the astronauts went through the awkward business of putting on their clothing, the great, clanking machine of Cape Kennedy on a launch day stirred to life around them. The rocket was already fueled and standing on the pad—6.2 million pounds of fuel and machine, plus an additional 1,200 pounds that were added all by themselves, as the humid Florida air condensed into frost along the skin of the rocket, which was chilled to freezing by the super-cooled liquid oxygen and hydrogen filling the fuel tanks inside.

On the Cape's beaches, the spectators emerged from their

tents and cars, blinking into the rising sun and training their binoculars on the rocket more than three miles away. Inside the sprawling firing room, 350 men sat at their consoles, manning a Mission Control far larger than the one in Houston. Yet this operation would be powered up for use only this morning; the moment the engine bells of the rocket cleared the launch tower and Houston took control, the firing room would have nothing at all to do with the flight.

When Borman, Lovell and Anders at last emerged from the suit-up building, they walked straight into a storm of flashing cameras and shouted questions from the reporters, who were held behind barricades to keep the crew's short path from the door of the building to the door of the transport van clear. The astronauts carried their portable air-conditioning units in one hand and waved with the other. They saw everything around them through the windscreens of their bubble helmets, and they heard the commotion caused by their departure mostly as muffled noise, like sounds from the surface world heard underwater. Once they climbed into the back of the van and the door was closed behind them, even that sound was stilled.

The drive to the pad was spent mostly in silence; so was the ride up the gantry elevator. As the Florida coastline fell away beneath the astronauts, the frosty, steaming flank of the rocket slipped by. The massive American flag decal and the capital-lettered USA and UNITED STATES—written vertically along the first and second stages—were visible through the ice layer, and the letters appeared in reverse order as the men rose higher.

At the top of the gantry came the walk along the caged

gangway of the swing arm to the white room, which surrounded the spacecraft. The hatch of the capsule—which looked for all the world like the one that had killed Grissom, White and Chaffee, even if it didn't function like it—stood open, waiting for them. Borman, who would fly in the left-hand seat, climbed inside. Anders, in the right-hand seat, climbed in next. Lovell, in the center and directly under the hatch, would be last, and thus he was left alone briefly on the swing arm.

He looked down at the ground far below and noticed for the first time the hundreds of thousands of people and cars—most with their headlights on in the predawn darkness—gathering to watch the liftoff. He noticed, too, that not a single one of those spectators had been allowed within a mile-and-a-half radius of the rocket. A circular, no-go footprint had been stamped around the massive, violent machine that was the center of so much attention. And the crew of *Apollo 8* was perched directly atop that machine.

"Maybe they know something we don't," Lovell muttered to himself—joking, mostly.

After making his way to the open hatch, he peeked inside and saw Borman frowning at the instrument panel. Little Christmas decorations hung in front of each seat.

"What is this?" Borman muttered as much to himself as to anyone else, though the question was audible through Lovell's headset.

"Guenter," Lovell responded, an answer Borman knew without having to be told.

Guenter was Guenter Wendt, one of the German engineers

who had come over with Wernher von Braun after World War II and now worked as white-room director and pad leader. Wendt was the last person each astronaut would see before the hatch was sealed, and he loved to surprise the crews with his little pranks and props. Plenty of the astronauts liked them, too—Wally Schirra, especially. But Frank Borman was no Wally Schirra, especially on a mission like this one, so he plucked off the decoration in front of his seat, looked back over his shoulder and gave Wendt a small and, he hoped, believable smile.

"Thanks, Guenter," he said, handing the nonregulation cargo back to him. Lovell and Anders did the same.

Now another member of the closeout crew appeared at the hatch. One by one, he stepped hard on each astronaut's shoulder, so they could tighten their seat restraints properly. The job had to be done just so, given the violence with which the crew would be shaken in their seats when the engines lit, then slammed forward during flight when the first stage cut off and dropped away, then slammed back when the second stage lit, and then back and forth again when the second stage gave way to the third. The hatch—the improved hatch that could be popped open in just a few seconds so that astronauts would never again be incinerated in their seats—was then closed and sealed. It would not be opened again until Borman and his crewmates had gone to the moon and come home.

More than an hour went by as the astronauts and the ground worked through their prelaunch checklists, which so far were being completed without any glitches. The more smoothly they went, the less the likelihood of any holds in the countdown and the sooner the mission would be on its way.

"*Apollo-Saturn* launch control," said Jack King, the broadcast voice of NASA.

When the astronauts had climbed into their spacecraft, the sun was barely up, but since then, the morning had brightened considerably. "T-minus seven minutes and thirty seconds and counting, and still aiming toward our planned liftoff time," King said. "Jim Lovell reported just a few minutes ago that he could see a blue sky and it looked like the sun is out."

The clock raced downhill toward the six-minute mark and the five-minute mark and then the four-minute mark. At three minutes, the tanks began to pressurize; a powerful churning, glugging sound filled the *Apollo* spacecraft, a much deeper tone than the one Borman and Lovell had heard in their little *Gemini* atop their *Titan* booster three Christmases ago. In the cockpit, Borman looked to Lovell, who nodded in recognition of the sound. Lovell then turned to Anders, who had no such sense memory, to offer a reassuring nod.

The last three minutes ticked off. When liftoff finally came, it was every bit as violent as it had been for *Apollo*s *4* and *6*.

"Liftoff!" Jack King announced as the five main engines erupted in their controlled firestorm.

"This building is shaking under us!" television anchorman Walter Cronkite called, once again delighting at the display of raw engineering power. "Our camera platform is shaking. But what a beautiful sight. Man is perhaps on the way to the moon if all continues to go well."

That generic "man," of course, was in fact three men, and for them the experience of liftoff was something else entirely. They were aboard the beast—within the beast—that was shaking Cronkite's building.

"Liftoff, and the clock is running," Borman called as loudly as he could over the roar. The clock on the instrument panel, which had been still while the clocks on the ground counted down, now began to count up.

"Roger. Clock," said Mike Collins, who would be manning the capcom for this mission.

"Roll and pitch program," Borman said, his voice shaking from the power of the 7.5 million pounds of thrust lifting 6.2 million pounds of machine. As it rose into the sky, the *Saturn V* began to orient itself, pointing its nose just so for the ride to orbit.

The noise inside the cockpit was like nothing the astronauts' simulator training had remotely been able to reproduce. For at least ten seconds—though to Anders it felt like the better part of a minute—the crew had no way to communicate with one another, which meant that each man would effectively be on his own in the event of an emergency. The g-forces were lighter than they'd been on the *Titan*, just over four, compared to the seven or eight Borman and Lovell had endured during the *Gemini* liftoff. But to Anders, the first timer, the *Saturn V*'s four g's felt like twice that number.

Anders was flabbergasted by the brute force of the *Saturn*. The engines at the bottom of the booster were designed to pivot one way or the other to keep the whole stack flying in the proper direction. But such minor motion at the base of the 363-foot rocket translated to violent thrashing at the top. Anders felt like a bug on the end of a whip.

The shaking in the cockpit was dramatically more severe than it had been on the *Titan*. Borman, as commander, had the responsibility of turning the abort handle that would carry the command module and the crew up and away from the *Saturn* in the event it went awry or threatened to explode. Mission regulations called for him to keep his gloved hand on the handle at all times, and he was not about to break any rule in the first three minutes of the flight. His fear, however, was that the powerful vibrations of the rocket could cause him to turn the handle by accident, ending an intended lunar mission just a few miles above the Atlantic. But as the rocket streaked into the heavens, Borman kept his hand steady.

At two and half minutes, when the *Saturn* and its crew were forty miles above ground and moving at 5,400 miles per hour, the first stage cut off and dropped away, punching the three astronauts forward into their restraints. When the second stage lit a second later, they were punched violently back into their seats.

For Anders, this whipsaw meant trouble. A few seconds earlier, he had tried to lift his hand toward the instrument panel and it felt to him as if a twenty-pound weight had been attached to it. The moment he did succeed in reaching forward was also the moment that the first stage cut out and the second stage lit, causing his hand to slam back into his helmet visor. The metal wrist ring left a nasty scrape across the unbreakable glass. He cursed himself—the rookie of the flight now had a big rookie mark on his faceplate.

Borman may or may not have seen Anders's mishap; if he did, he exercised the commander's prerogative to ignore a small screwup. "The first stage was smooth and this one is smoother," he announced to the ground.

"Roger, smooth and smoother," Collins answered. "Looks good here."

At the eight-minute mark, the trip suddenly became less smooth, as the *Saturn V*, now shorn of its first stage, began the vibrational bouncing that had nearly torn *Apollo 6* apart.

Borman frowned again. "Picking up a slight pogo here," he said.

"Roger, slight pogo," Collins echoed, both men wondering why von Braun's newly installed dampers and shock absorbers weren't doing their jobs. But seconds later, the equipment proved itself, working whatever bit of mechanical magic it possessed to settle things back down.

"Pogo's damping out," Borman said.

"Understood," Collins said.

And with that, the *Saturn V*, which had caused so much worry, did every single thing von Braun had built it to do without another instant's trouble. Its second stage cut off and fell away just when it was supposed to; its third stage lit briefly and shut down again, providing just enough of a kick to carry *Apollo 8* to a temporary parking orbit around the Earth. The spacecraft's orbit was too low to sustain for an extended mission, but it was perfectly fine for a crew that would not tarry long. While taking some bearings and checking their systems, the astronauts would make less than two circuits of the Earth before firing up their third-stage engine once more to light out, at last, for the moon.

Lovell settled back into his seat, then spoke to his crewmates. "OK, we can breathe a little bit more, hear a little bit more, huh?" Around him, the stray dust and occasional bolt left behind by the technicians again floated up into view.

"That was quite a ride, wasn't it?" Borman answered, easing back as well.

"Felt like an old freight train," said Anders.

"It *is* an old freight train, pal," Lovell said, snapping off his gloves and taking off his helmet. "Let's get comfortable. This is going to be a long trip."

On that point, Lovell was exactly right. The moon, at the moment of launch, was 233,707 miles from Earth. At the very peak of their current orbit, the *Apollo 8* crew still had 233,604 miles to go.

NINE

December 21, 1968

TECHNICALLY, GENE KRANZ did not need to be present at Mission Control in Houston on the day *Apollo 8* launched. The official manning list—the roster of every controller who would sit at every console for each of the three eight-hour shifts during the six-day flight—did not include Kranz's name anywhere. His odd-on, even-off flight schedule had him busy not with the business of flying *Apollo 8*, but with planning for *Apollos 9, 11, 13, 15* and on down the line for however long the moonships kept flying. For *Apollo 8*, the prime seat in Mission Control— the flight director's console—would be filled by a rotating cast, consisting of Cliff Charlesworth, Milt Windler and Glynn Lunney, and they would be more than up to the job without Kranz there to second-guess their work.

But what the manning list said and what Kranz wanted were two different things, and for him, Mission Control was the only possible place to be. Kranz loved everything about the great high-ceilinged control room, with its big board of maps and data filling the front wall like a giant movie screen.

Kranz could be dropped into Mission Control at any point

in any flight and sense, just by looking around the room, how far into the shift and into the flight plan the controllers were. He could tell by how full the wastebaskets were, how stale the sandwiches looked. He could tell by whether the pizza was congealed or steaming, by whether the coffee smelled fresh or burned.

If things were going well, most of the men would be tending to business at their own consoles. If there was a problem, a huddle would have formed around the relevant console. One huddle meant one problem. More huddles spelled what could be real trouble.

On the morning *Apollo 8* launched, even a novice would have sensed that all was going smoothly. Kranz arrived well before liftoff and took a seat near the back of the room, where he could observe unobtrusively but be available immediately if he was needed. As the countdown clock ticked toward zero, there was the usual bracing; as the *Saturn V* roared to Earth orbit, there was the usual tension. Once the rocket arrived there, the controllers would have nearly three hours before the next big milestone—translunar injection, or TLI, the engine burn that would send the astronauts moonward.

TLI was a tricky business, involving lighting up the engine on the third stage of the *Saturn V* that was still attached to the spacecraft. The third stage was nearly the height of a six-story building and when it fired, the engine would accelerate *Apollo 8* to the proper speed to put it on its way to the moon. The third stage would then be jettisoned and sent into a waste-disposal orbit around the sun. It all looked simple enough in the equations and simulations, but it had never been tried in crewed flight before. And its success depended on a team of men sitting at different consoles covering varied areas of expertise, all coordinating their efforts. Still, if anyone in the room was feeling anxious about attempting the maneuver, they weren't showing it.

A relaxed-looking Mike Collins was working the capcom console. Collins was the right man to have on-shift at the beginning of the flight, since this particular crew probably knew him better than any other astronaut in the corps. Chuck Deiterich was at the Retrofire console, to manage the procedures in which the ship turned its blunt end forward and lit its SPS engine to enter the moon's orbit, then later exited the moon's orbit and, finally, reentered the Earth's atmosphere. Jerry Bostick was at the flight dynamics, or FIDO, console, where he managed the craft's trajectory. They were two more crew favorites and two more good choices, since the TLI burn would be in their hands.

Best of all would be the sight of Flight Directors Charlesworth, Windler and Lunney. They were three men doing the same job, but each had to be deadly serious about what the flight directors called "chasing nits"—noting any tiny glitch in the performance of any system, glitches that might make no difference at the moment but could, for the next director at the same point in the next mission, be critical.

Kranz looked around at the solid team in the humming room and then turned his attention to the great display screen with the familiar, flat map of the Earth and the track of an orbiting spacecraft inscribed around it. Soon enough—shortly after TLI—that map would change. For the first time in history, it would switch from a circular route to a translunar route, with the Earth on the left-hand side and the moon on the right and a spacecraft slowly creeping from one end of the board to the other. And then, in less than three days' time, the map would switch again, this time to an orbital map of the moon.

Something, Kranz felt, was about to shift, something bigger and grander than one space flight or one victory in the Cold War with the Soviets. He looked forward to the exhausting business of being back on the console for all the flights to come. But today he was happy to have less to do. The change this mission would work on the world would be too beautiful to miss.

✳ ✳ ✳ ✳ ✳ ✳ ✳ ✳

Somewhere between ninety-nine and one hundred and three miles above the Earth, Frank Borman, Jim Lovell and Bill Anders were not thinking such soaring thoughts. They were, for the moment at least, thinking about not throwing up. Borman and Lovell were hardly strangers to space. Borman had spent fourteen days there; Lovell, the world record holder for time aloft, had logged eighteen. But they had spent all of that time sealed inside a *Gemini* spacecraft, and its ninety-one cubic feet of habitable volume did not even permit a man to get out of his chair. Yes, they had been weightless, but they knew it was mostly because the things around them floated, not because they did themselves.

The *Apollo* capsule was different. It didn't just have a comparatively spacious two hundred and eighteen cubic feet, similar in size to the interior of a large car, it had two hundred and eighteen *smart* cubic feet, configured in a way that allowed for maximum mobility even with three men competing for the room. There was enough clearance between seats and instrument panel for the astronauts to float over one another easily, getting from section to section or window to window with ease.

The capsule also had what was known as a lower equipment bay beneath the foot of the couches. As its name suggested, the bay was partly used for stowage, but it was also where the navigation console was located, meaning that the bay operated as an entirely separate workstation, distinct from the instrument panel. It was even big enough to provide a little privacy if an astronaut wanted to take a nap or needed to use a waste disposal bag. Those, regrettably, had not improved since *Gemini*.

Once the crew got to orbit, Lovell was the first to open his seat belt and pop out of his couch. He drifted down to the equipment bay to stow his helmet and promptly felt his head swim and his stomach turn over. Taking hold of a solid ledge on the spacecraft wall, he held himself steady.

"Be very careful getting out of your seat," he called back up to Borman and Anders. Anders looked quizzical, but Borman, who had talked with Lovell about the possibility of space sickness in so big a ship, knew exactly what Lovell meant.

"Look straight ahead for a while," Borman said to Anders. Then he opened his seat belt, too, floated down to join Lovell and felt the same sickly swoon. He remembered the steak-and-eggs breakfast he'd wolfed down that morning and fought to keep the food down where it belonged. Anders, feeling cautious now, stayed where he was for a few moments before unbuckling as well.

Motion sick or not, in the brief two laps around the Earth the astronauts would have a lot to do before the ship was fit for TLI. Borman's job on this mission was the job of any commander, which meant he was fluent in every single system aboard the spacecraft, could fly the ship alone if he had to and bore the weight of command as well. He would have the final word on anything and everything that happened over the next six days.

Lovell had been tapped as navigator, and given that *Apollo 8* would travel much farther than any other craft in the history of space exploration, that was no small responsibility. While the computer had all the coordinates it would need for the flight stored on magnetic tape, that mechanical brain still needed a human brain to confirm what the machine thought it knew before the main engine or even a single one of the sixteen smaller thrusters could be fired.

Both the computer and Lovell had the location of thirty-five stars committed to memory. These navigational coordinates were every bit as accurate—and every bit as primitive—as they were for the sailors who used them centuries ago. Lovell would need that knowledge whenever the ship had to make a maneuver of any kind, and there would be a lot of them. He was also the keeper of all the computer's other commands, especially the firing instructions that would be used when the main engine would make its critical burns. If there was a crew member who would call the lower equipment bay home for much of the six days ahead, it was Lovell.

Anders's role was somewhat improvisational. Part of his responsibility would be to serve as mission photographer, a job that was far more important than merely serving as *Apollo 8*'s history-keeper. The reason for orbiting the moon a full ten times was not only to take the gravitational measure of the dangerous mascons, but also to get three sets of eyes and some first-rate film cameras scoping out possible landing sites for the missions to follow. And he would take as many photos as his many rolls of photographic film could hold.

Until the time to do that work came, he would also oversee the command module's life-support systems. It was straightforward enough work—monitoring oxygen, heaters, water flow and more—though it came with little margin for error. The very term "life-support systems" made clear what would happen if those systems failed.

Now, as Anders unbuckled, he surveyed his meters and immediately spotted a problem. The pressure indicator on the glycol system that was supposed to cool the instruments was way too low.

"Boy," he said, partly to himself, "it's way down there. Something's fishy."

"We'll take a look," Borman said, running the spacecraft's schematics in his head. "Are we in primary?" Borman asked, referring to the setting on the instrument panel, as opposed to a setting that read the secondary, or backup system.

"Oh, we're in secondary." Anders flicked the switch to its proper setting. "It's okay."

Borman drifted over, glanced at the indicator and smiled as the pressure rose to normal. The error was harmless, both men knew. All the same, Anders was annoyed at himself. This kind of blunder never would have happened if he'd been flying his LEM.

This wasn't the only mistake early in the mission. None of the three men had yet removed the yellow life vests they wore during liftoff, a safety precaution in case they had to end the mission on the way into orbit and ditch in the ocean. As Lovell floated past the base of Borman's seat while checking on the navigation panel, his life vest's activation lever caught on a protruding rod. A loud pop and hiss sounded and the vest began billowing up on his chest.

Lovell looked comical, but the situation was not. Under normal circumstances—on Earth, in other words—it would be easy enough to deflate and stow the life vest. But the vest had been inflated by a small canister of pressurized carbon dioxide, and releasing a big blast of CO_2 in a small, enclosed space with a limited supply of breathable air was not a good idea. The spacecraft was equipped with air scrubbers—square canisters the size of a large cookie tin filled with crystalline lithium hydroxide that would absorb CO_2 before it could build up to dangerous levels. But, like sponges, the canisters would eventually become saturated and then have to be swapped out with a fresh one. Dirtying up the first filter on the first day of the mission was a bad way to begin.

In short order, Lovell figured out an elegant solution. He floated over to the closest thing to a proper bathroom the spacecraft had—the urine station in the lower equipment bay. Like the system aboard the *Gemini*, the station was nothing more than a tube attached to a funnel at one end and a small reservoir in the wall at the other. The urine would flow from the astronaut, through the tube and into the reservoir. A twist of a knob would then vent the unwanted liquid into space, where it would flash freeze into Schirra's spangly Constellation Urion.

Lovell removed the funnel from the end of the tube, opened the life jacket valve, fitted it in its place and then vented the CO_2 invisibly overboard. When he was done, he folded the vest and stowed it in the storage area. Over the next six days, all three men would have to move around the small cabin a lot more carefully, but the mission's first serious problem was solved.

✳ ✳ ✳ ✳ ✳ ✳ ✳ ✳

The TLI burn that would propel the *Apollo* out of Earth orbit and orient it toward the moon's orbit awaited the astronauts exactly two hours, fifty minutes and forty seconds into their mission—near the end of their second Earth orbit. It would require extraordinary precision. For that reason, neither the astronauts nor the onboard computer would execute it. Instead, the burn would be directed by the room-size computers at Mission Control.

The way the physics works, flying away from Earth is more like climbing uphill from Earth, with the ascending power of speed battling the downward pull of gravity. Take off going a little too fast and you're going to win that tug-of-war—but if you miscalculate and miss the moon, you'll fly off into space and be adrift forever.

Slowing down just a bit too much means you will ultimately lose that gravitational battle, so if your trajectory is far off and you miss the moon entirely, you will simply arc over and head back home like a ball thrown high in the air that falls back to the ground. If you miss the moon by only a little, you'll be moving slowly enough to surrender to the moon's gravity, at which point you'll whip around the far side and get hurled back to Earth. In the first case, you'll make a U-turn in empty space; in the second case, you'll speed around the traffic cone of the moon. Either way, you remain on what flight planners called a free-return trajectory—and either way, you'll be heading home, never having entered the moon's orbit.

Until the burn took place, Lovell, for one, was content to claim a few minutes of downtime and drift from window to window while reacquainting himself with the singular view of the Earth, slowly turning below his spacecraft. It was a vista he'd seen over the course of 330 orbits the first time he was in space; he would see it for a far briefer spell on this flight, but especially since *Apollo* had five windows to *Gemini*'s mere two, he wanted to make the most of his opportunity.

"Gee, this is the best flight I've ever had," he said with a wink to Borman, a comradely reminder of the grind the Gemini 7 mission had been. He looked out the window again and caught a bright flash as the nighttime side of the Earth gave way to the day. "Here comes the sun," he announced.

"Where?" asked Anders, eager to see as many sunrises and sunsets as possible during their brief stay in the Earthly neighborhood.

"Well, take a look," Lovell said, waving him over to the window. "It crept up on us."

Though Borman stole a few glimpses of his own, he was not partial to the idea that his crew would spend their limited time in orbit sightseeing. But since they were so busy with the windows, he reckoned that he might as well put them to work there. Given how central lunar mapping was to the mission, a lot would ride on keeping the multipaned windows clear, and that would not be easy. Any moisture clinging to the exterior windows that had been carried up from Earth would flash freeze in the vacuum of space.

"Let's give Houston a window status report as far as contamination," Borman ordered. And so they did, reporting on specks of dust or smudges that shouldn't have been present.

"You're looking good, *Apollo 8*," Mike Collins said. "We don't have anything for you. We are just standing by."

The remainder of the standby time ticked slowly away. To avoid bothering the crew, Collins held his tongue; instead, he listened to the chatter on Mission Control's internal loop as the other controllers confirmed that the computers and guidance system and third-stage tank pressures were all what they should be. Finally, twenty-three minutes before the critical burn, Charlesworth, who was in the flight director's seat for this first shift, gave Collins the high sign: it was time to signal the astronauts that their ship was fit to leave home. Collins nodded.

"All right, *Apollo 8*," he said. "You are go for TLI. Over."

"Roger," Borman answered, his voice without inflection. "We understand we are go for TLI. Over."

Collins sat back in his seat. He was startled to discover

that what should have been one of the most thrilling moments of his life was actually one of the most unsatisfying.

Three human beings, he reflected, were about to tear themselves away from the close gravitational grip of Earth, and in three days' time they would surrender to the gravity of another celestial body. No living creature had ever done that before. There ought to be an oompah band. There ought to be fireworks. There ought to be *some* way to mark the moment. Instead, there was just this dull, flat little scrap of language: *You are go for TLI.*

But the jargon was deliberate: it was designed to hollow out those very feelings of momentousness, because feelings like those could be distractions when you needed to focus only on the task at hand. Elsewhere in Mission Control, Jerry Bostick, at the flight dynamics console, allowed himself a flicker of the forbidden wonder.

"They're leaving us," he muttered to no one in particular. "We've got these guys headed out of orbit."

In the spacecraft, Borman and his crew did what the flight plan directed, which was to return to their couches and buckle their restraints. There would be no need for anyone to stand on their shoulders; this time, the belts would simply prevent them from drifting out of their seats. Once the engine was lit, the acceleration would create just enough gravity to settle them back in place.

"All right, gentlemen," Borman said to Lovell and Anders, "let's get set for this."

The astronauts scanned their instruments and saw nothing amiss in alignment or fuel pressure or anything else. Then, just as their training called them to do, they scanned their instruments again. All seemed in order.

At the five-minute mark before TLI, Collins called the crew. "*Apollo 8*, Houston," he said. "You're looking good down here. Everything looks good."

"Roger, understand," Borman answered.

As those final five minutes melted away, the spacecraft and the ground held their silence as best they could.

"*Apollo 8*, Houston, coming up on twenty seconds till ignition," Collins said, his eyes on the clock. "Mark it," he called out. "You're looking good."

"Okay," said Anders.

"Roger," said Borman.

Lovell gave Anders another encouraging smile, then turned to Borman, who did not glance back. The commander's eyes were fixed on the instrument panel clock and the ignition light next to it.

"Nine, eight, seven . . . ," Borman announced, then counted in his head for a digit or two. "Four, three, two . . . ," he resumed.

Behind them, the crew felt a rumble. Fifty-nine feet away, the liquid oxygen and liquid hydrogen flowed from their separate tanks and mixed in the combustion chamber. As the ignition system engaged, the exhaust exploded out of the third-stage engine bell—silent in the vacuum of space, it created a low, vibrating rumble inside the spacecraft.

"Light on," Borman called. "Ignition."

"Roger, ignition," Collins said.

The expected shadow of gravity nudged the crew from

behind. Instruments throughout the command and service module, tuned like seismographs to every change in velocity or orientation of the spacecraft, twitched in reaction to the sudden acceleration, turning what they recorded into digital signals and displaying them on the instrument panel. Far more precise sensors—written into the brains and vestibular systems of the astronauts themselves, the result of years and years of flying—reacted, too.

"Boy, it's going off in yaw," Borman said, not liking a slight slewing to the side that both his gut felt and his alignment indicators confirmed.

"It's okay, the DAP is fine over here," Anders said, referring to the digital autopilot.

Lovell was busy minding the other axes in which the spacecraft could drift. "What's your attitude at—" Lovell began to ask.

Anticipating the question, Borman cut him off. "Fine, forty-five . . ."

"OK," Lovell said.

"And the tank pressure?" Anders asked.

"Tank pressures are good," Borman said.

"OK," Anders answered.

For five minutes and twenty seconds, the men alternated between silence and necessary chatter. The engine burned and the ship slowly began to climb that gravity mountain from the Earth to the moon.

Now toward the end of the burn, it was Lovell's job to keep his eyes fixed on the instrument panel clock. He called off the three-minute, two-minute and one-minute marks to shutdown.

"Thirty seconds to go," he called.

Then: "Ten seconds. Really fine."

Then: "Five, four . . ."

He trailed off.

Finally, three seconds later, just as suddenly as the engine had roared to life, it went completely still. The only sound that filled the cockpit now was the whirring of the cabin fan, the breathing of the three men and the crackle in their headsets from the command center. Yet they were leaving the Earth behind at an unheard-of 24,200 miles per hour.

"Okay, we got SECO right on the money," Borman said as casually as if he were announcing that he'd just picked up the mail.

"Roger," Collins said, "understand SECO."

The moment was marked. Once again a bit of chill jargon—meaning "sustainer engine cutoff," or shutdown of the spacecraft's big motor—stood in for whatever emotions the men had been born to feel but had fought and trained not to feel.

In Mission Control, Gene Kranz, exercising the privilege of the spectator, allowed himself to feel plenty. Standing at the back of the room, he watched as the big map on the wall changed: now it showed the long journey ahead. Three men had broken away from the planet. The first mission to the moon had officially begun.

TEN

December 21, 1968

VALERIE ANDERS CHOSE to watch the launch of *Apollo 8* in the way that made her most comfortable—which was to say in no special way at all. She would not sit in the VIP stands on the space center grounds, among a crowd of celebrities and the family members of NASA's astronauts. She would not smell the rocket fuel or feel the ground shake or have to shade her eyes to follow the *Saturn*'s rise into the sky. Instead, she would sit on a wooden toy chest in the family den with her youngest child in her lap, the rest of her children at her feet and a television set in front of her. What the moment might lack in drama, it would make up for in comfortable familiarity.

This would by no means be the first launch Valerie and her family had watched on TV in their den, but it would be the first they watched on a *color* TV. The Anderses had been among the last families in the neighborhood to trade up to that particular luxury. But given that this would be Bill's first flight and that he'd be away from his family on the very week practically every other family in the country would be gathering together, Bill decided he ought to leave a special gift behind—especially if it would allow his family to have a better view of the beginning of his adventure.

Hours before launch, the Anders home began filling up with astronauts and their families. So did the Borman home, and the Lovell home would do the same once Marilyn and her children got back from the Cape.

But early that morning, the focus was on the television. Watching a *Saturn V* fly on-screen may have been nothing like watching it fly in person, but it was still very dramatic. You could sense its massive size, and even through the tinny speaker of an ordinary TV, you could hear its explosive roar. As Valerie watched the five main engines light—in full, living color—and saw the rocket rise and heard Walter Cronkite shout about his booth shaking and man perhaps being on the way to the moon, she had only one thought: "Thank you, Dr. von Braun."

It was odd maybe, but it was apt. He had built the rocket, and that rocket, she could already tell, was flying true. She stayed to watch the *Saturn* do its job, shedding its first stage and dwindling to a dot. She watched as the TV animations took over to show the parts of the mission the cameras no longer could. She heard the reporters announce that her husband was in orbit around the Earth. And then, less than three hours later, she learned that he had left that orbit and was headed for the moon.

Valerie knew she would need to take the mission as a series of such moments and milestones, and that she'd have to pace herself emotionally—and pace her children, too. This was especially important since they would have to spend so much of the next six days inside the house.

The day before, she had planned to drive over to the space center's little food store to get some supplies for what she knew would be a week of siege. A few journalists had already arrived and taken up positions in front of her house; by launch morning, the crowd of reporters and photographers would grow large enough to encircle the house, effectively imprisoning her family inside.

To avoid the early-arriving journalists, Valerie had tried to slip out of the house through the children's playroom door, which opened on the backyard and was concealed by a wooden fence surrounding the property. Carrying Eric, the youngest, who at four years old would still suck his thumb if he was feeling tired or overwhelmed—both of which he was feeling today— she worked the gate open with her free hand. As soon as she'd done so, she walked straight into a photographer. He snapped a picture of an ambushed mother and a startled-looking toddler who had just popped his thumb out of his mouth.

"Thumbs up for Dad!" the caption under the photograph in the next day's paper would read.

Valerie, defeated even in that small venture outside, retreated indoors to begin her confinement early. Before long, she realized that she needn't have worried about going shopping. By that evening, her refrigerator was stuffed with casseroles and sandwiches and potato salad and snacks, and her counters were stacked with pies and coffee cakes and cookies, all provided by the visitors who had been through this experience before and would never think of coming to the Anders home without a platter of food.

If there was a measure of privacy to be had, it came from an accommodation NASA always made for the astronauts' families: a small squawk box that was typically set up in a bedroom or some other less-public spot. From the moment the crew took off until the moment they splashed down, the device allowed the family to listen to every second of the air-to-ground chatter, though NASA built an extra couple of seconds into the transmission, allowing for a kill switch to spare the families from hearing something they shouldn't. Nobody in Mission Control who had heard the voices crying out from the burning *Apollo 1* spacecraft could abide the idea of that kind of horror pouring straight into the ears of the dying man's wife or child.

Before Bill left, he had been honest with Valerie about the risks he faced and the odds that he would ever come home. Planning for every possibility, he had left behind two tape recordings for the children. They were to listen to the first tape on Christmas Day; they were to listen to the second tape only if it became clear that the family would never again spend Christmas together.

Valerie gave as little thought as possible to that second tape. She was a pilot's wife and she had long since developed a kill switch of her own, one that allowed her to consider only the things she could control and ignore the terrible things she couldn't. Many of her friends were pilots' wives, too, and a number of them had husbands in Vietnam—a very different, far bloodier battle than a mission to the moon. If they could shut out the fear, she could do it, too. What's more, she would help her children learn the trick as well.

She knew she could not promise her children that their father would come home, and therefore she wouldn't. But she could promise them that they had her, and that they always would.

"I'm here," she told them as she tucked them into bed the night after the rocket was launched. "And I'll be here." She planned to repeat that every night until Bill was back.

✶ ✶ ✶ ✶ ✶ ✶ ✶ ✶

Susan Borman's sons did not need to be reassured the way Valerie Anders's children did—or if they did need it, they weren't about to show it. To the boys' great relief, and winning their enduring gratitude, Susan and Frank didn't force them to engage with the NASA press machine. Fred and Ed pursued their own interests away from the media's glaring eye. Sure, what dad was doing was a very big deal, but they had high school to deal with and their own teenage lives to lead. Fred was now seventeen and Ed was fifteen, and both were taller than their five-foot, eight-inch father. They were tall enough to be on the high school football team, which they were, and tough enough for it, too. And they were old enough to believe that there were emotions a man displayed and emotions he didn't, and they guessed they knew the difference.

The boys got their innate calm from their father, but they got another kind—the kind you could put on even if you weren't feeling it—from their mother. There were days when Susan and the boys needed that skill more than others, and *Apollo 8*'s launch day was one of them. Friends and family began arriving before dawn, and Susan stayed busy entertaining her guests, keeping watch over her sons and sparing them the peckings of the press. There were no reporters in the house during lift-off, but after *Apollo 8* was safely in space, she gave them what they needed—on her terms—emerging on the front lawn with Frank's parents and the family dog, and without Fred and Ed. After the cameras finished capturing that tableau, she offered up a few words.

"I'm always known as the person who had something to say, but today I'm speechless," she said.

But then she did speak, answering the predictable questions with the proper declarations of confidence and pride. Finally, toward the end of the brief session, she said, "I'm too emotionally drained to talk."

Then, begging the press's pardon, she went inside. She had a very long week ahead and knew by now exactly how much attention she could spare for the reporters on any given day. For launch day, she had no more to give them.

✳ ✳ ✳ ✳ ✳ ✳ ✳ ✳

Before the astronauts of *Apollo 8* had even shed their heavy pressure suits and donned the white jumpsuits they would wear throughout their mission, they had already traveled farther from Earth than any person ever had. By the time they reached the thirty-minute mark after the TLI burn they were climbing to 12,000 miles.

Apollo 8's spectacular altitude should have meant an equally spectacular view of the Earth, but the crew couldn't yet think about turning around the spacecraft to get a good look at their home planet. For the moment, the more important issue was that the *Saturn V*'s third stage was still hanging off the back of their service module. The rocket's final stage had done its job well, but now it was space junk and it had to go.

The third stage was connected to the spacecraft by a ring of explosive bolts. The separation maneuver called for the crew to detonate the bolts, then pulse their thrusters to add a few extra feet per second to their speed. That would open a gap between the spacecraft and the third stage. And the gap couldn't be small, either: when the bolts blew, the stage would begin leaking stray fuel through severed lines, making its behavior unpredictable—the last quality you want in a 23,000-pound piece of hardware that's trailing right behind you. Borman wanted no part of that kind of randomness.

Each of the astronauts had a part to play in the delicate maneuver. Anders would have the flight plan checklist in hand and read off the separation commands; Lovell would punch them into the computer and execute the explosive separation; Borman would control the thrusters once the spacecraft was free. Lovell, for one, had been looking forward to this first opportunity to operate the computer in flight: he had spent many hours practicing with the powerful electronic brain on the ground, and now it was finally time to test it for real.

The computer, which had a nine-button keypad, was relatively compact, but it had a very large screen that was able to display twenty-one characters in a single line from left to right.

The language of the machine was, in its way, a great deal like spoken language, consisting principally of verbs and nouns that were represented by numbers. During months of training, Lovell had made it his business to learn how to speak the computer's language fluently. A verb represented some action that was to be taken, and a noun represented the thing that was supposed to be acted upon. Punch in the verb "82," which stood for Request Orbital Parameter Display, and the computer would digest the command and then wait for more. Which orbital parameters exactly? Inclination? Velocity? There were a lot of them. Following the "82" with a "43"—for latitude, longitude and altitude—would complete the command and the computer would respond. Fortunately, the complex separation maneuver would be made somewhat easier because part of the procedure was preloaded, which meant the computer had all the nouns memorized. All Lovell needed to provide were the verbs.

Borman scanned his instrument display to make sure the ship was configured properly for the maneuver. It was.

"All right," he said with a nod at his crew.

"Okay, verb 62, enter," Anders read out.

"Verb 62, enter," Lovell confirmed and punched the proper key.

"Verb 49, enter," Anders said.

"Verb 49, enter," Lovell repeated.

Anders scanned his instruments and nodded in approval. "Okay," he said, "proceed."

"Roger," Lovell answered and pressed the button on the display panel that read just that: PROCEED.

The bump that occurred when the bolts exploded took all three men by surprise. It was certainly tolerable, especially compared to the earthquake of the launch, but it was much more of a punch in the back than the simulations had led them to believe it would be.

Borman shook off the jolt, grabbed the pistol-grip handle that fired the spacecraft's thrusters and began edging forward so that the crew could look through the windows to check their distance. Borman fired his jets, performed the half somersault and looked out his window. Nothing. He nosed left, then right; up, then down. Still nothing.

After another moment, Lovell called out. "There it is!"

"You found it?" Borman asked.

"Right in the middle! Right in the middle of my window!"

The third stage was there all right—bright white and reflecting the sun. By eyeball reckoning, it appeared to be as far behind their spacecraft as the computer said it was, which was several dozen yards, but that was not yet far enough. Borman could see that it was spraying so much fuel that it was in danger of tumbling. Looking at it, and not liking what he saw, Borman began contemplating whether an evasive maneuver would be necessary.

Then, suddenly, all thoughts of the troublesome third stage fell away, because in that moment he saw something much, much grander. He saw the Earth.

It was a view that American astronauts and Soviet cosmonauts had seen from space many times before, but in those cases, the planet had been a broad arc, too big to fit into the frame of a window because it was too close. Now, however, Borman, Lovell and Anders were seeing the planet floating alone, unsupported, in space. The Earth was no longer the soil beneath their feet or the horizon below their spacecraft. It was an almost complete disk of light suspended in front of them, a delicate Christmas-tree ornament made of swirls of blue-and-white glass. It looked impossibly beautiful—and impossibly breakable.

What Borman said aloud was: "What a view!"

What Borman thought was: *This must be what God sees.*

Then he collected himself. "We see the Earth now, almost as a disk," he radioed down.

"Good show," Collins said. "Get a picture of it."

Borman gestured to Anders, but it wasn't necessary; the mission photographer was already assembling his cameras. Lovell looked out the window and described the scene Anders would capture.

"We have a beautiful view of Florida now," he said. "We can see the Cape, just the point. At the same time, we can see Africa. West Africa is beautiful." Then, to stress the magnitude of what he had just said—the perspective he had—he added, "I can also see Gibraltar *at the same time* I'm looking at Florida." More than that, he could see Cuba, Central America and most of South America. "All the way down through Argentina and down through Chile," he said.

Borman allowed himself to take in the view for a moment longer, then turned his mind from sightseeing back to business. No matter how NASA had expected third stage to behave at this point in the mission, it clearly wasn't playing along. It was supposed to leak only a little fuel and then conduct what was known as a blow-down maneuver, emptying whatever remained in its tanks in a quick and tidy blast. But Borman was not seeing anything like quick and tidy now.

"Houston, *Apollo 8*," he radioed down. "I suggest a separation maneuver if that's all right with you."

There was silence on the ground. Borman could practically see the flight controllers contemplating this idea, conferring with one another about whether to green-light so routine a procedure as an unplanned thruster firing. He gave them about twenty seconds to consider the matter.

"Houston, *Apollo 8*," he repeated.

His words were again greeted with silence. This time he gave them just six seconds.

"Roger," he said with finality. "I believe we're going to have to thrust to get away from this thing."

There would be no dithering on his command. He hit his thrusters and *Apollo 8* jumped quickly away from the third stage, leaving it to fall into its trash-can orbit around the sun.

✳ ✳ ✳ ✳ ✳ ✳ ✳

If the global audience that was following the mission during its first twenty-four hours had been listening carefully, at least a few of its members might have noticed a troubling bit of chatter going on between the spacecraft and the ground. It's a safe bet that no one actually noticed; there was too much else to pay attention to as the spacecraft blew through its 12,000-mile altitude record, increasing it tenfold to 120,000 miles in the time it took the Earth to turn just once.

Even more exciting was the promise of several live TV broadcasts from space. The first was due to occur at the thirty-one-hour point in the mission—or about 3:00 p.m. Eastern Standard Time on December 22—when the folks at home could see the planet they inhabited from the same surreal perspective enjoyed by the astronauts.

Still, there was that occasional troubling chatter. To the uninformed listener, it would almost certainly be merely puzzling.

Anders, for instance, could say: "Houston, we've rewound the tape. You can dump it at your convenience."

And Collins would respond: "*Apollo 8*, Houston. We're going to try to dump your tape right now."

A while later, one of the astronauts would say that NASA might enjoy some interesting details on those tapes, and then he would request that NASA let the crew know their opinion of the tapes once they'd had a chance to listen to them.

What the crew and the ground were talking about was the DSE, or data storage equipment, which was more casually known as the dump tapes. Installed in *Apollo 8*'s cockpit was a recording system that remained on, more or less continuously, from liftoff to splashdown. The dump tapes recorded everything the astronauts said to one another in the privacy of their spacecraft, without the air-to-ground loop picking up what was being discussed. Not only did the tapes create an important historical record, they also provided critical information if there were ever an accident on board and a later investigative committee had to determine the cause of the problem.

Most important was that the taping system gave the crew a way to record a private message to Mission Control and then transmit it at high speed without anyone in the larger world listening in. But Mission Control would need to find a spare moment to listen to it, and at present they were taking their time about doing so. That was a problem, because what the crew wanted the ground to know was that Borman was sick—and it wasn't just the mild motion sickness that Lovell and Anders had experienced early on.

For the better part of twelve hours, Borman had been alternating between throwing up and battling the urge to throw up, a fight he often lost. He was also experiencing intermittent episodes of very loose bowels, which often accompany this kind of digestive upset. Both problems were far more difficult to manage in a spacecraft that had no indoor plumbing. Although the commander was going about his work and his voice betrayed nothing, he could carry on that way only for so long. If Borman couldn't eat food and hold it down, his performance would falter and eventually he wouldn't be able to function. Already, the sound and smell of his suffering were making the cramped cockpit unbearable for all three men. Worse, if Borman's sickness was caused by a virus, Lovell and Anders would almost certainly contract it, too.

At first, Borman forbade the crew to breathe a word to the ground. But after half a day, Borman himself was worried. During *Gemini 7,* his stomach had been rock-steady for fourteen straight days. This time, however, his digestive system was in full revolt.

Lovell and Anders knew that if he had to, Borman would just grind it out, and that worried them. But finally they persuaded him to sign off on the dump-tape plan, which would eventually bring the problem to the attention of the flight surgeon, Dr. Charles Berry—or so they hoped.

Hours after the recorded transmissions had been sent, Houston at last picked up the hints the crew was sending and folks on the ground listened to the tapes with mounting alarm. The best case was motion sickness. The not-good case was a virus. The worst case—the one that occurred to Berry immediately— was radiation sickness. It was consistent with the sudden onset; it was consistent with the vomiting; it was consistent with the diarrhea. And on this mission, a ready source of radiation poisoning had been impossible to avoid: the Van Allen belts, the bands of radiation that surround the Earth from a low of 400 miles up to a high of 36,000 miles.

The *Apollo 8* crew had plowed right through the belts, getting a full dose of the high-energy rays, with little to stop them but the comparatively thin skin of the spacecraft itself. Even at the high speed the ship was traveling, the crew would need two hours to clear the upper limits of the radiation field.

Berry had been fretting about the risks the Van Allen belts posed since the beginning of the Apollo program, but there was no way off the planet Earth except to push through those thousands of miles of radiation, so they had built the most robust ship they could and hoped the crew would not suffer any ill effects. Now, Borman was displaying exactly the right symptoms at exactly the right point in time.

Berry raised the radiation poisoning possibility to the flight directors, but they weren't persuaded. *Lovell and Anders were healthy, weren't they?*

So far, Berry answered.

And even if the belts extended more than 35,000 miles high, they reminded him, *the radiation dose was low all the way through—little more than what a man would get from a chest X-ray.*

Yes, Berry replied, *a two-hour chest X-ray.*

Still, Berry was a scientist, and he had to agree that if the other two astronauts were not experiencing Borman's symptoms, it was unlikely that radiation sickness was causing the commander's distress.

The likeliest explanation, to his way of thinking, was a virus, and that would create a serious situation. According to flight rules, that left him only one option.

"I'm recommending that we consider canceling the mission," he said.

The flight directors looked at him in disbelief. But also according to flight rules, their only option was to get on the radio and send the medical man's opinion up to the ship. Still in the backup control room, they called the crew and got right to the point.

"Dr. Berry thinks you've caught a bug, and he's worried Bill and Jim are going to get it, too," the capcom Mike Collins said to Borman. "He's recommending that we consider canceling the mission."

"*What?*" Borman exclaimed. He turned to Lovell and Anders, equal parts amused and outraged by the suggestion. Looking at his crewmates and lowering his voice to a mutter, he said, "That is pure, unadulterated garbage." The other two men nodded in agreement.

For Houston's benefit, Borman collected himself. "Look, you've got three mature people in a spacecraft here, and we're not just going to turn around and come home. I'm fine." That was hardly the case, but he then amended his fib with the truth: "Or at least I'm feeling better."

And in fact he was. The half day it had taken him to admit the problem and the additional half day it had taken NASA to respond to the dump tapes had given his stomach time to settle. Now Borman was sure the problem wasn't radiation, and he suspected it wasn't a virus. That left the most pathetic explanation of all: motion sickness. He was the first American astronaut ever to report it, but in the roomy *Apollo*, he suspected he wouldn't be the last. Either way, he would speak of it no more.

✷ ✷ ✷ ✷ ✷ ✷ ✷ ✷

The reception was terrible on the one television in the office inside the Central Research Institute building in Moscow. There were other channels to watch—much clearer channels—but they were all state-controlled. If you wanted to get European television, which was what the men in the office needed today, you had to rig a special cable. That was certainly something the engineers who worked in a place like the Central Research

Institute building could manage, but it didn't mean the picture would be terribly good.

Still, that was the only way the Soviet space officials could follow the activities of the three men aboard the American spacecraft that was now, just thirty-one hours after its launch, half-way to the moon and about to beam a television show to Earth.

Top Soviet officials and engineers had watched the Americans take off the day before on a giant viewing screen in Building 88 of the nearby Scientific Research Institute, and the sight of the bright white *Saturn V* had been discouraging enough. The Soviet Union's own *N-1* rocket—the military green heavy-lift vehicle that was their answer to the *Saturn*—had not yet had a successful uncrewed flight, much less a crewed one, and here were the Americans trusting the lives of three astronauts to their cursed *Saturn*.

The television show from inside the spacecraft would make them feel even worse, with the happy, cocky Americans showing off for their countrymen back home—and showing up the people of Russia. For that reason, there would be no more big-screen viewings in Building 88. Unless folks could figure out how to rig the cables, TVs in the Soviet Union would stay dark.

When the broadcast began, the sloppiness of the whole affair was impossible for the Soviets to miss. The three Americans may have been on the way to the moon, but they didn't appear to be taking the job very seriously or doing it very well. The astronaut they called Anders was holding the camera, and he seemed not quite able to make the thing work. He tried to show the Earth out the window, but the exposure was all wrong and the image came through as a washed-out circle.

"We are having no joy," said a voice from the space control center in Houston, in apparent criticism of the astronaut's work.

"How about now?" Anders asked.

"Still no joy. It's coming through as a real bright blob. Hard to see what we're looking at."

The camera then swung around to show the inside of the ship and the picture became much better. The commander known as Borman appeared on the screen, but he was upside down.

"You have everybody standing on their heads down here," said the voice from Houston again.

"Well, we all have our problems," answered Anders. Then he turned the camera and righted the picture.

The commander began talking. "I certainly wish that I could show you the Earth," Borman said. "It is a beautiful blue with predominantly blue background and just huge covers of white clouds."

The camera moved again and showed the third man, Lovell, in what looked like a storage area beneath the seats, working with a plastic packet of some kind. "Jim, what are you doing here?" said the commander. Answering his own question, Borman said, "Jim is fixing dessert. He is fixing up a bag of chocolate pudding. You can see it kind of floating by."

Lovell smiled and looked toward the camera, already showing a growth of beard after only a day and a half without a shave. The commander noticed that, and said, "Let everybody see that he has already outdistanced us in the beard race. Jim has quite a beard already."

Anders appeared on the screen, and as he handed the camera off to Borman, he picked something up.

"You can see Bill has his toothbrush here," Borman said. "He has been brushing regularly." Then Anders began playing with the toothbrush, letting it go and catching it in the air. "To demonstrate how things float around in zero-g," Borman explained. "It looks like he plays for the Astros, the way he tries to catch those things." Presumably, this was a reference to an American sports team.

The men went on like that in their happy way for five minutes or so, before ending the transmission. "We will be signing off, and we will be looking forward to seeing you all again shortly," said Borman.

"Roger," said the voice from the control center.

"Good-bye from *Apollo 8*," said the commander.

The transmission from space ended, both for audiences watching it in the free world and for anyone who managed to get a signal somewhere else. The next day there would be a much larger meeting in Moscow's Central Research Institute building—the little television show had made that certain. Dimitri Ustinov, the future Minister of Defense, would chair it, and he would ask a question that would surprise no one.

"How are we going to respond to the Americans?" he would demand. "Sort it out and tell me what you're going to do."

Nobody attending the meeting was likely to have a very good answer.

ELEVEN

December 22, 1968

ON THE SAME day the men in Moscow were sullenly watching the broadcast from *Apollo 8*, others in the Soviet bloc were also turning their eyes toward the mission. The little show from deep space might not have been carried anywhere in the Soviet Union or Eastern Europe, but official blackouts were only so effective and plenty of people knew that with a little artful rigging of a powerful antenna, they could pluck a forbidden signal straight out of the air. There may not have been many broadcast pirates, but more than a few of them reported what they had seen. In the West—and pretty much every other place on the planet that could pick up a television transmission—the show from the spacecraft was widely available. Though the first broadcast from *Apollo 8* almost certainly did not break any records, the networks concluded that the global audience exceeded one hundred million viewers, and it was possibly two or three times that.

They watched the five-minute show in Britain, where the *Sunday Times* admitted, "the *Apollo* flight is thrilling us all." They watched it in France, where the *Journal du Dimanche* called the flight "the most fantastic story in human history." They watched it in Hong Kong, where broadcasts from Britain's BBC were readily available even if mainland China was ignoring the mission. "HONG KONG MAN ON WAY TO MOON," read the headline in more than one newspaper, delighting in Anders's geographic birthplace, while overlooking the fact that a child born on an American military base was legally born on American soil.

Hours before the broadcast, Pope Paul VI, in his weekly address to the crowds at the Vatican, had *Apollo 8* on his mind, too. "We accompany with our prayers the courageous astronauts, flying in space at a dizzying speed, wishing a happy success to a risky interplanetary voyage," he said.

In the US itself, all three television networks carried the show, and they fully intended to air every minute of the five other broadcasts from space that NASA had arranged. And why wouldn't they? The ghostly signal showing three ordinary men with ordinary names like Frank and Jim and Bill making an extraordinary journey was an entirely different kind of news from the full-color, close-up bloodshed that had been filling TV screens all year. It was a wholly good thing in an unhappy year.

But whether the run of luck would hold for the three men in the small pod hurtling through the deep void would not be known for a few more days.

✳ ✳ ✳ ✳ ✳ ✳ ✳

As far as the people in NASA's public affairs office were concerned, there was entirely too much conversation about balls and urine going on between the *Apollo 8* astronauts and Mission Control.

Ship-to-shore communications were always a scratchy business, which was why call signs or vectors that included letters like "A," "C" and "T" became "Alpha," "Charlie" and "Tango" for clarity. The same thinking applied to the use of "balls." Numbers had no rhymes that could cause problems, so it was fine to call out "one," "two" and "three" by their proper names. But "zero," which was even less likely to create rhyming difficulties, proved to be an irresistible target, and so aviators referred to zeros as "balls."

For *Apollo 8*, the word went out that "balls" would return to a gentleman's "zero." Still, habit was habit and aviators were aviators, and over the course of the mission a few "balls" were still slipping through.

The talk about urine posed a more difficult problem. It went deeper than mere language; besides, there was no way to avoid talking about it. Newton's laws of motion—particularly the ones about objects in motion tending to remain in motion and all actions having equal and opposite reactions—may have been all that was needed to get a spacecraft moving toward the moon and then keep it going even after its third stage engine had completed its work. But maintaining a true course took a little more effort.

The giant main engine—the SPS—provided a booming 20,500 pounds of thrust, and each of the sixteen little reaction control thrusters produced one hundred pounds. But physics makes no distinction between forces you want and forces you don't, and a fine mist of urine or other wastewater venting from the side of the spacecraft could provide a tiny thrust of its own.

It wasn't an issue anyone worried about during the carousel ride that was Earth orbit, but on what was supposed to be a straight shot to the moon, even a tiny nudge off course at the beginning of the trajectory could mean a huge error at the end. Already, less than forty-eight hours into the mission, the guidance officers were noticing a slight drift in *Apollo 8*'s path. As a consequence, they were regularly discussing with the astronauts how and when to schedule their urine dumps.

In some ways, Chris Kraft was glad for the development. He very much wanted to test the engine, and an SPS burn to correct the drift in trajectory provided the perfect opportunity. In Kraft's view, it would be recklessness of the first order if the spacecraft arrived at the moon without ever having tested the main engine that would be needed to get the crew into and out of lunar orbit. If there was an issue with the engine, it was best to know that now, and have a couple of days to deal with it, than for the astronauts to learn about it only when they tried to fire the SPS on the far side of the moon, a point at which they would be completely out of radio contact with Houston. After listening in on the trajectory chatter from his observer's console at the back of the firing room, Kraft strode up to what was known as the trench—the front row of consoles where the flight dynamics and guidance officers sat—to make his preferences known.

"We need that SPS engine to work, and I very much want to see it burn before we go behind the moon," he announced.

Then he turned and left the trench, and the engineers set about doing the only thing they could do—whatever Kraft told them. They ran the numbers for the maneuver and found that it would be an almost absurdly minor exercise. The necessary course correction would require a pulse of the SPS lasting slightly longer than two seconds.

Still, Houston called the maneuver up to the ship and the astronauts prepared to execute it. Anders, sitting in his right-hand seat, read off the steps for a burn from the flight plan, and Lovell, in the equipment bay, punched them into the computer—knowing, from the months of simulations, what Anders would read off before he actually did it, but abiding by the call-and-response rules that governed any burn of the engine. Borman, in the left-hand seat, counted down. Then the engine lit and the ship bumped forward; 2.4 seconds later, the exercise was over.

"Like a big spring," Borman said, surprised at the sudden lurch, but otherwise shrugging it off.

Kraft reacted very differently. The second the engine was lit, he saw an anomaly in the data. It was exactly the sort of problem he'd feared, exactly the reason he'd wanted a burn. It didn't look like much unless you knew exactly how the data was supposed to look, and Kraft did know. The problem, an issue with the flow of chemicals, was minor enough that they could have overlooked it, but the entire point of their jobs was to see everything and overlook nothing. Actually, this brief SPS burn cleared out the problem as it properly purged leftover helium from the lines. Now the fuel lines would be entirely clear. Kraft nodded in satisfaction, cast a stern look at his trench controllers, and returned to his observer's console. Observing every single thing going on in the room was exactly what he would continue doing until the three astronauts were safely home.

✳ ✳ ✳ ✳ ✳ ✳ ✳ ✳

Nobody expected the *Apollo 8* command module to be anything like a pleasant place throughout the mission, given that three grown men would be confined in it for six full days. But no one expected it to get quite so ripe quite so fast. Borman's space sickness had gotten the journey off to a disagreeable start, and things had gone pretty much downhill since then.

Urine dumps would still be made as needed, but with the trajectory to worry about, the exact meaning of "as needed" would change. No longer would the wastewater be vented outside as soon as it left the astronaut's body; instead, the urine would be stored in sealed plastic bags. But the bags were never sealed quite well enough to prevent the singular smell, if not the liquid itself, from leaking out. And for every bag that was filled and stored, the odds that one of them would be bumped and ruptured increased.

The stuffiness inside the ship was another problem. The temperature on any one part of the exterior skin of the spacecraft varied from about 200 degrees below zero to 200 above, depending on whether that section of the exterior was facing the glare of the sun or the deep freeze of shadowed space. To keep things balanced, the spacecraft would spend most of the flight in what was known as passive thermal control—or PTC—mode. This was nothing more or less than a slow, one-revolution-per-minute rotisserie roll that would be initiated with a single burn of the thrusters and would continue indefinitely until there was a counter thrust.

But inside, the cabin temperature hovered at about 80 degrees, thanks mostly to the sunshine streaming periodically into the windows. The spacecraft had heaters, but beyond a fan to circulate the interior atmosphere, there was nothing to cool the air.

The astronauts' personal equipment had problems, too. Their slipper-like boots began to fray almost immediately after they put them on, and Borman and his crew worried that a loose thread could snag on something or throw a switch inadvertently. So they shucked the booties and got by with their socks. Then there were the headsets. When the astronauts were sealed in their pressure suits for liftoff, they wore black-and-white fitted hoods under their helmets, with the earpieces and microphone built right in, nicknamed "Snoopy hats" after the popular beagle in the *Peanuts* comic strip. They were supposed to use ordinary headsets, which would be less hot, for the rest of the trip, but those had proven impossibly glitchy, so it was back to the black-and-white fitted hoods. The Snoopy hats may have cost them a measure of dignity, but they gained them a lot of function.

Getting adequate rest was often an issue for astronauts, but fortunately both Borman and Lovell found that sleep came relatively easily. In the *Apollo* spacecraft, many of the operations were automated, so Houston allowed the astronauts to sack out simultaneously if they wanted, and the lower equipment bay included sleeping bags that could be rigged like hammocks.

But Borman did not care for the idea of simultaneous sleep shifts. It felt like negligence, like falling asleep at the wheel of a speeding car, even if there was nothing remotely nearby to hit and no accelerator or brake to mind. So on the second night in space the commander forced himself to stay awake while Lovell and Anders slept. At about the forty-hour point in the mission—it was 11:00 p.m. in Houston—Jerry Carr, who was manning the capcom console, tried to keep Borman company, chatting about the weather and the news.

Then Borman fell silent and looked out his window. The home planet, so much farther away than it had been during the first broadcast, hung before him.

"Boy, Jerry, that Earth is sure looking small."

"Roger," Carr answered. "I guess it'll get smaller, too."

Borman smiled. "Yes," he answered softly, "we're getting along pretty good."

✳ ✳ ✳ ✳ ✳ ✳ ✳ ✳

About eight hours into *Apollo 8*'s third full day in space a remarkable milestone would be reached. The crew wouldn't see it happen and they wouldn't feel it happen—they'd still be soaring silently through space with more than a half a day to go before they reached the moon—but it would happen all the same. At precisely fifty-five hours, thirty-nine minutes and fifty-five seconds mission-elapsed time, the astronauts would cease being people of the Earth and instead become people of the moon.

By the time the spacecraft passed the 200,000-mile mark, the power balance between the parent planet and its little moon would shift. At that point, the increasing pull of lunar gravity would at last overcome the greater, but fading, pull of Earth's gravity, meaning that the uphill march would become a downhill plunge, and the spacecraft's speed would once again begin increasing. After that moment, it was physically inevitable that *Apollo 8* would at the very least whip around the far side of the moon. Perhaps the crew would succeed in entering orbit; perhaps their engine would fail them and they would be tossed back home by lunar gravity; perhaps the engine would overburn and they would crash into the moon. But whatever happened, Borman and his crew would become the first humans in the history of the species to see the lunar farside.

✶ ✶ ✶ ✶ ✶ ✶ ✶ ✶

Several hours later, it was time for *Apollo 8*'s next broadcast. Tuesday at 3:30 p.m. would normally be a poor slot for any TV show, but it was December 23—schools were closed and plenty of businesses were already shuttering for the holidays.

Progress in the mission meant progress in the quality of the pictures the crew was able to send home. The planet outside the spacecraft's window was still grainy and without color, but a proper polarizing filter sharpened the image considerably, as did simply holding the camera still. This time, the blurred picture of the Earth seemed almost to sizzle into focus.

Before the broadcast began, Borman fired his thrusters to stop the rotisserie roll so that Anders, who would be handling the camera again, could fix it squarely on the Earth. Then Borman looked out at the view and was struck by what he was seeing.

"We are looking at the Earth right now and there is a spectacular, long, thin band of clouds," he said. "It's absolutely spectacular, going all the way—or almost halfway—around the Earth."

"Roger, we would like you to repeat that during the TV narrative," Collins said, "and we would like you, if possible, to go into as much of a detailed description as you poets can possibly muster."

Poetry would not be quite what the audience would get today. But if the people viewing the broadcast looked hard and squinted properly, the slightly better picture made it possible actually to see the clouds and landforms of Earth that the astronauts were describing.

When the show began, Lovell played narrator. "What you're seeing," he said, "is the Western Hemisphere; at the top is the North Pole."

After allowing that information to register, he continued. "Just lower to the center is South America, all the way down to Cape Horn."

After another pause, he said, "I can see Baja California and the southwestern part of the United States."

Whether the audience could actually make out the shapes described by Lovell wasn't the point. It was the fact that they had the chance to try, to see their home planet from a remove of 200,000 miles and make of it what they could, just as the astronauts were doing.

Exactly as Houston wanted him to, Lovell went on to talk about the Earth's colors, describing where the brown of desert gave way to the blue of water and the white of clouds. Then, at least a little transported by it all, he gave the ground a bit of the poetry it had requested.

"What I keep imagining is if I am some lonely traveler from another planet, what I would think about the Earth from this altitude," he said, "whether I would think it would be inhabited or not."

"Don't see anybody waving, is that what you're saying?" joked Collins. After having asked for the lyricism, he now seemed to be laughing it off.

But Lovell would not be denied a whiff of wonder. "I was just kind of curious if I would land on the blue part or the brown part of the Earth," he mused.

"You better hope we land on the blue part," Anders said.

"So do we, babe," Collins answered.

Lovell smiled and went back to the more straight-up work of describing without reflecting. Privately, however, he decided that he was at that moment about as happy as he'd ever been.

The broadcast finished about seventeen minutes after it began. Before long, Collins called up to them once again. "By the way," he said, "welcome to the moon's sphere."

shower up, make their own breakfasts and come back later in the morning.

For Fred and Ed, breakfast gave them a chance to enjoy some brief private time and eyeball their mother to detect how she was holding up. The answer, they could readily see, was not terribly well. As always, she took good care of her guests and smiled gamely for the press, so her picture in the papers looked fine if you didn't really know her well. But Fred and Ed could read her face better than almost anyone else, and everything from the tight set of her mouth to the spooked look in her eyes spoke to them of a kind of knotted terror.

Fred, as the older son, took it upon himself to ensure that he and Ed behaved this week. *Let's not act like knuckleheads* was the way he liked to put it. But the bigger problem was the simple matter of boredom, with every second of every day filled with nothing but moon talk. Having grown up with the space program, they knew no other life, and it took a lot to get them excited. They had watched the *Apollo 8* launch along with the adults, but when the time for the burn out of Earth orbit arrived, they drifted from the room. They could hear their father's voice coming through the squawk box or the TV, and during the two broadcasts back to Earth they wandered into the living room, got a peek of him on the screen—he was growing a beard, but with his sandy hair it was less noticeable than Jim Lovell's and Bill Anders's dark scruff—and then wandered back out.

When they could, they left the house and went over to their friends' homes, where there were no crowds and no newsmen and the TV might not be on at all. "Going out," Fred would shout to Susan as they were getting ready to leave, taking care not to go into the living room, where they would have to say good-bye to a dozen people they hadn't even said hello to earlier that morning.

"Not the front door!" Susan would call back, an unnecessary reminder that the front yard was jammed with press.

The backyard was safer, surrounded by a high fence with a door that had a sturdy latch, which meant that unlike Valerie Anders, the boys had no reason to fear that a cameraman would be waiting to ambush them. And if the boys suspected that someone was lurking on the other side of the door in the fence, they would avoid it entirely, vault the farthest stretch of fence, and take the back streets to their friends' homes.

When they arrived, an adult would inevitably ask about the mission, to which they had little to say.

"Not really thinking about it," they would answer.

And if anyone raised the topic of the danger their father faced—which too many people seemed inclined to do—Ed would remind them who they were talking about.

"Dad's in the air force," he'd say, "a lieutenant colonel. There's a cold war going on."

Ed Borman was still only in high school, but he sounded so much like his father when he said such things that the adults who heard him could only shake their heads.

Their father, off fighting that war, would have approved.

✳ ✳ ✳ ✳ ✳ ✳ ✳

Anyone who hoped to mark the moment when *Apollo 8* entered lunar orbit would likely be disappointed. The spacecraft was set to arc behind the moon at 3:50 a.m. Houston time in the first few hours of Christmas Eve day, breaking the communications link between the spacecraft and Mission Control that had been maintained since the astronauts had climbed into their ship three days earlier. As long as there is nothing between a spacecraft and the Earth, astronauts are in radio contact. But the moon is in the way when you're on its far side and radio waves can't penetrate it. On the screens in Houston it would be as if the *Apollo 8* spacecraft and its crew had simply vanished into space. The data stream would be reduced to nothing—all balls—and only a translunar hiss would fill the headsets.

The communications blackout would last about thirty-five minutes. Ten minutes into it, the astronauts would fire their engine for the Lunar Orbit Insertion (or LOI) burn, and that either would or would not make them satellites of the moon. Until they emerged back into the storm of radio waves streaming from their home planet, nobody on that planet would know if the three men were dead or alive.

The engine burn that would settle the matter one way or another would have to be executed very precisely. As the spacecraft made its final approach before loss of signal, or LOS, its 3,800-mile-per-hour speed would increase to 5,800 miles per hour thanks to the pull of the moon's gravity. The ship would be flying backward, with the engine bell facing forward so that the burn could act as a brake, like paddling your canoe backward in a fast-moving river, bringing the speed back down to

3,700 miles per hour. That was slow enough for lunar gravity to grab the ship and settle it into orbit sixty nautical miles above the moon.

Those were the nice round numbers that NASA gave the press, but the astronauts and the Mission Controllers preferred to work in units that were more precise, reaching far to the right of the decimal point. They had a tiny margin of error—the equivalent of standing at one end of a football field and shooting at an apple in the opposing end zone—but aiming to skin it, not hit it.

For the astronauts themselves, the final approach to the moon would be an exercise in flying more or less blind. They hadn't glimpsed the moon since their first day in space, when they had been traveling nose forward.

"As a matter of interest," Lovell called down at 2:50 a.m. Houston time, an hour before loss of radio contact, "we have as yet to see the moon."

As the time to loss of signal and the Lunar Orbit Insertion burn slowly ticked away, both the crew and the ground attended to minor housekeeping chores, confirming communications settings, cockpit recorder status, trajectory details and the like. But it was really little more than busywork, a way to remain occupied during the final approach to the moon.

Finally, at sixty-eight hours and four minutes ground-elapsed time, the capcom gave the crew the official approval for the mission's riskiest moment, the maneuver on which the entire voyage depended.

"*Apollo 8*, Houston," Carr said, "at 68:04 you are go for LOI."

"Okay, *Apollo 8* is go," Borman answered.

Carr sat uneasily in the silence that followed. As Collins had found, the cold jargon of the capcom was simply not up to the magnitude of what he had just given the crew the clearance to do.

"*Apollo 8*, Houston," he finally added. "You are riding the best bird we can find."

"Thank you," Borman replied. Then, five seconds later, he added a small bit of sentiment of his own. "Roger, it's a good one."

As if on cue, Mission Control's big map on the wide screen in the front of the room changed: after showing the translunar route for the better part of the past three days, it switched to a lunar map. The path the spacecraft would follow if the burn went well was traced across its surface.

"*Apollo 8*, Houston, we have got our lunar map out and ready to go," Carr told Borman.

"Roger," Borman said.

After that, there was little chatter until about forty-five minutes later, when Carr once more hailed the ship.

"*Apollo 8*, Houston," he said. "Five minutes till LOS; systems go, over."

"Thank you," Borman answered. The static crackled, and then Carr spoke up again.

"Frank," he said, "the custard is in the oven at three fifty."

"No comprendo," Borman said.

And then, an instant later, he did understand. It was a message from Susan, who, if he knew her at all, would be keeping the house together and keeping the guests looked after, and would, as the loss of signal and engine burn approached, also be listening to the squawk box alone somewhere, in the kitchen perhaps, maybe in the bedroom, with no one beside her to see her relief if things went well or her devastation if they didn't. As Susan knew, public displays of powerful emotions were simply not how things were done.

Still, she could send Frank a message. So she had spoken to Carr when he was off-shift and asked him to radio up the coded declaration of family solidarity, her promise to him that she would let him handle the risky business of flying if he would let her handle the household and the children.

Now Borman smiled—a small, private smile. Perhaps Anders caught it, perhaps he didn't. Either way, he answered for his commander, preventing Carr from repeating the message and spoiling whatever its secret sentiment was.

"Roger," Anders said.

Shortly afterward, Carr announced the one-minute mark to LOS. Then, with only seconds remaining, the man at the capcom microphone spoke the words everyone else in the control room was thinking. "Safe journey, guys," he said.

"Thanks a lot, troops," Anders answered.

"We'll see you on the other side," Carr called.

A moment later, at exactly the second NASA had calculated, the signal cut out.

The men in the spacecraft looked at one another partly in wonder, partly in admiration.

"That was great, wasn't it?" Borman asked. With a laugh, he added, "I wonder if they just turned it off."

Anders liked the joke. "Chris probably said, 'No matter what happens, turn it off,'" he added.

Chris Kraft had said no such thing, of course, and the *Apollo 8* crewmen knew it. As the long thirty-five minutes of radio silence began, the three astronauts were disconnected from the rest of humanity in a way that no one ever had been before.

✴ ✴ ✴ ✴ ✴ ✴ ✴ ✴

Gene Kranz stood at the back of Mission Control. Ship-to-shore contact would be briefly lost on occasion, silences that were predictable and familiar, and carried no special weight. But no ship had ever gone into the blackout that was caused by flying behind the 2,159-mile-wide bulk of the moon, and this silence felt different.

Chris Kraft, sitting at his observer's console near where Kranz was standing, took the opportunity to pour himself a cup of tea. He walked over to the table where the hot plate and coffeepots were kept and stood next to Bob Gilruth, not only the first director of the Manned Spacecraft Center in Houston but one of the original members of the Space Task Group, the committee established by President Eisenhower in 1958 that led to the creation of NASA.

"Ten years and a month," Gilruth said. "There were thirty-six of us on the list, including you, Chris."

"And now we've got three men behind the moon," Kraft answered. "If we weren't sitting here, I don't know that I'd believe it."

Both men gazed at the mission clock in the front of the room. The length of the blackout was not absolutely fixed. If all went well, it would last about thirty-five minutes—a bit longer if the engine fired successfully and the ship slowed to 3,700 miles per hour and settled into orbit, a bit shorter if the engine failed to fire and the ship continued to speed along at 5,800 miles per hour. If something worse happened, the men behind the moon would never emerge.

✷ ✷ ✷ ✷ ✷ ✷ ✷ ✷

Inside the spacecraft, the astronauts were too busy to spend a lot of time thinking about all the possibilities facing them. The burn was less than ten minutes away and there was a lot to configure before the ship was ready.

The final configuring was supposed to take up four or five of the ten minutes that remained, but the crew had drilled the procedure so many times on Earth that they completed it in just two of those available minutes.

"Okay, eight minutes," Borman said, glancing at the countdown clock.

Lovell looked around him. His crewmates did not seem tense, but they didn't seem especially relaxed, either. "Well, the main thing is to be cool," he said.

He gave the radar indicator a look. With the spacecraft windows facing up and the ship pointing backward, the astronauts still couldn't see the moon. But the instruments knew that it was now directly beneath them.

"Well, I'll tell you gentlemen," Lovell said, "that moon is pretty close."

"Seven minutes," Borman said.

Borman squinted out the window and frowned. There was still only blackness. "On that horizon, boy, I can't see squat out there," he said.

"You want us to turn off your lights and check it?" Anders asked, reaching for the interior lighting switches.

Before he could touch them, however, Lovell called out, "Hey, I got the moon!"

"You do?" Anders asked.

"Right below us!" he said, looking through his window.

And indeed, there it was, just visible through Lovell's backward-facing window. The ship had now traveled far enough past the leading edge of the moon that some of the ancient, gray surface stretched beyond the *Apollo*'s nose. The expanse was huge—a ruined, meteor-blasted beach that spread out to the right and left until it spilled over the horizons.

Jim Lovell, the first human being in history to see it, stared transfixed and said nothing.

"Is it below us?" Anders asked excitedly, pressing close to his window.

"Yes, and it's—" Lovell began.

"Oh my God!" Anders exclaimed.

"What's wrong?" Borman said.

But nothing was wrong. Anders was now seeing the moon for himself. "Look at that!" he said. "I see two—" He waved his hands to fill in the word *craters*, which, in his excitement, was eluding him. "Look at that!" he repeated.

"Yes," Lovell said.

"See it?" Anders said. "Fan . . . fantastic."

"All right, all right, c'mon," Borman scolded, minding his ship while his crewmen gaped. "You're going to be looking at that for a long time."

"Twenty hours, is that it?" Anders asked, knowing full well that ten two-hour orbits would mean they'd be looking at the moon for a total of twenty hours. All the same, he seemed eager to reassure himself of his sublime good fortune.

Anders and Lovell settled back into their couches, and then all three men loosely fastened their seat belts to keep secure when the engine fired.

"One minute," Borman said. Then he added, "Come on, Jim, let's watch it real good."

Lovell would do exactly that, since it was his job to work the computer keypad on the instrument panel and punch in the final commands for the four-minute engine burn. He checked the altitude and velocity readouts he was being fed by the computer and then entered the commands he had practiced a thousand times in simulations.

With ten seconds to go, he consulted the computer readout one more time. It flashed "99:20" back at him. That was the computer's last-chance code, its way of confirming that the human being at the switch really did want to do what he was about to do.

When the countdown clock reached zero, Lovell hit the button marked PROCEED.

Somewhere behind the astronauts, the engine bell began emitting a silent roar of exhaust, slowing the ship down in its backward-facing position. Borman, Lovell and Anders heard none of that, but they felt it in the form of a subtle pressure at their backs.

"One second, two seconds," Borman read aloud as the first moments of the 242-second burn played out. "How's every—"

Anders, anticipating Borman's question, responded to it before he could finish. "We got them. Pressure's holding good."

"Fifteen seconds," Borman said.

"Pressure coming up nicely," Anders assured his commander.

"All right."

"Everything is great."

The engine burned on and the ship continued to slow, fighting ever so slightly the tug of the moon's gravity so it could properly settle into lunar orbit. At least that was the plan.

"Four minutes?" Borman muttered as they approached the two-minute mark.

"Longest four minutes I ever spent," Lovell said, after nearly another minute had elapsed.

As the engine continued to burn, the astronauts could increasingly feel its effects with the pressure at their backs turning into a shadow of gravity. It was less than a single g, but for men who had been weightless for three days, it felt like much more.

"It seems like about three g's," Anders said.

Lovell kept his eyes on the clock and announced when there was just one minute left, then forty-eight seconds, then twenty-eight seconds.

"Stand by," he said.

"Okay," Borman answered.

"Five, four, three, two, one," Anders read off.

And then, right on schedule, the SPS—the Service Propulsion System that had served, and propelled, and had now slowed the spacecraft, too—went silent.

"Shutdown!" Borman announced.

"Okay!" Lovell said with a satisfied nod.

In that moment, *Apollo 8* became a satellite of the moon. The spacecraft was circling it in an elliptical orbit with—as the ship's instruments confirmed—a high point of 169 nautical miles and a low point of just sixty, or precisely the parameters Houston had planned. And the three astronauts now orbiting the moon were the only people on or off the world who knew they had succeeded.

✳ ✳ ✳ ✳ ✳ ✳ ✳

The silence in Mission Control stretched on, as the idle people at the consoles tapped their pencils and jiggled their feet. Many of the controllers stared at the mission clock in the front of the room. With their console screens still receiving no information at all from the ship, the clock was the only functioning data point left. So they watched it tick down.

Thirty-four minutes and two seconds after the spacecraft disappeared into blackout, Carr began hailing the ship.

"*Apollo 8*, Houston. Over," he said, knowing that it was a bit too early to expect an answer, but not too early to hope for one.

"*Apollo 8*, Houston. Over," he repeated thirty-three seconds later.

"*Apollo 8*, Houston. Over," he repeated after fifteen more seconds.

He said it yet again after eighteen more seconds, and then thirteen more seconds and then twenty-three seconds.

At last, eight seconds later—thirty-five minutes and fifty-two seconds after LOS—the lifeless crackle in the controllers' headsets was replaced by something that was very much alive.

"Go ahead, Houston, this is *Apollo 8*," said the unmistakable voice of Lovell. "Burn complete. Our orbit 160.9 by 60.5."

"*Apollo 8*, this is Houston. Good to hear your voice!" Carr answered.

In truth, the capcom barely heard a thing, since all the men around him had leapt up as one, whooping, cheering, and embracing one another in relief and jubilation. The display went way beyond what Mission Control decorum permitted. But nobody cared: decorum was lost and that was just fine. Paul Haney, the NASA commentator who was narrating the events for the early morning broadcasts, made the obvious official.

"We got it! We've got it! *Apollo 8* is now in lunar orbit," he shouted over the din. "There is a cheer in this room!"

It was much quieter in the kitchen at the Borman home, where Susan, as Frank suspected, had been waiting out the long lunar silence alone. But even there, the cheers from her living room were impossible not to hear.

* * * * * * * *

America awoke slowly to the news that three of its countrymen were in orbit around the moon. The predawn hour of the orbital burn meant that most of the people living in the nation that had sent the spacecraft on its journey were not awake when Lovell spoke the words so many had been waiting to hear.

In much of the rest of the world, which was considerably deeper into its day, the response was different. Television networks all over Western Europe interrupted their morning and afternoon broadcasts with news from the moon. The Netherlands had a special hunger for the story, and even the radio stations that usually broadcast only music suspended or interrupted their programming to carry regular updates on the mission. Iran's state-controlled television network covered the story steadily and live, as did Tehran's main radio station. In Libya, a nation that had been established seventeen years prior to the day, huge rallies celebrated both the country's independence and *Apollo 8*'s astonishing feat. Accounts of the successful orbital maneuver were even reported faithfully in the Soviet Union. The news was not announced there until an hour and fifteen minutes after *Apollo 8* sailed back around the near side of the moon, but by the standards of the state-run Soviet press, that was almost as good as live.

✳ ✳ ✳ ✳ ✳ ✳ ✳ ✳

If the crew of *Apollo 8* hoped to take some time to reflect on their remarkable circumstances, they would have to do so during the quiet intervals while circling the far side of the moon. For each of their spacecraft's ten orbits, the astronauts would be in radio contact with the ground for nearly ninety minutes, and during those intervals there would be too many chores to attend to and too much chattering in their ears. Worse, a TV broadcast had been planned for the first orbit on the near side of the moon, meaning that hundreds of millions of people would be listening to and watching the goings-on in the ship. Americans who missed the broadcast due to the early hour would be able to see it on what would be a near-continuous loop throughout the day.

During the first few minutes of blackout after the orbital burn, the astronauts thus allowed themselves what they knew would be the brief luxury of mere sightseeing. The flight plan called for the spacecraft to roll over and fly upside down for most of its twenty hours in lunar orbit, since upward-pointing windows would be useless if you were trying to map the moon that lay below. Borman executed a series of thruster maneuvers to spin the ship around, filling the windows with nothing but moon. All three men peered out, and at first all three men said nothing.

Nearly 4.5 billion years earlier, a passing protoplanet had collided with the infant Earth, knocking it to the cockeyed 23-degree tilt that would one day give it its seasons. The collision sent up a great debris cloud that, for a short time, gave the planet a ring. Within a few eons, the ring coalesced into a moon. That new satellite would soon become gravitationally locked to the Earth, meaning that it would always keep one side facing its parent planet and the other side pointed out to space. Less than a billion years after the moon formed, the first one-celled organisms appeared on Earth. It would be another two and a half billion years before multicelled organisms, some with rudimentary light-sensitive eyespots, followed, and on dark nights those spots may have registered the photons pouring down from the brightly lit moon. Later, other organisms with better eyes—and in one case, a mammal with a big brain and opposable thumbs and a consuming curiosity about the nighttime sky—would come along, too. And in all of that time, not a single human eye had ever seen the side of the moon that the six eyes belonging to the astronauts in the *Apollo 8* spacecraft were seeing now.

Those men were there on a mission, and if they were given to wonder, which they surely did, they kept it mostly to themselves. But it was evident in their tone and in the long silences between their words. Those words, however, were mostly about the job they were there to do, which was to understand the science, not gawk at the spectacle.

"Boy," said Lovell softly, blinking at the bright light of the sun, which was still directly overhead and reflecting off the lunar surface. "There's no shadows in those craters at all."

He scanned back and forth across the surface, comparing the huge, dusty world he was seeing with the two-dimensional maps and photos taken by telescopes and lunar satellites he had been studying for so many months. Almost immediately, Lovell knew where he was. "We're passing over Brand right now," he announced, recognizing the forty-mile-wide crater that had been informally named for rookie astronaut Vance Brand, who had been on *Apollo 8*'s support crew and had earned himself a little recognition.

Then—bigger, more brilliant—came a one-hundred-mile crater, one of the most conspicuous features left over from one of the most violent hits the lunar farside had ever sustained. "Is that Tsiolkovsky?" Lovell asked no one in particular, knowing full well it was. Studying maps of the moon and not being able to recognize Tsiolkovsky Crater would be like studying maps of the United States and not recognizing Florida. But Lovell was asking anyway, less out of confusion than out of simple incredulity that he was here at all.

He and Borman continued to scan the ground rolling slowly below, picking out other craters, too: Scaliger, Sherrington, Pasteur, Delporte, Necho, Richardson. Once just cartographers' marks on flat pieces of paper, they were now solid formations of dirt and rock and ancient lava flows, the entire history of the moon written in its wounds. Meanwhile, Anders began bouncing around the cockpit, excitedly collecting his lenses and cameras and film magazines.

"I've got Mag D," he said, after darting down to the equipment bay and grabbing some film. "And this lens," he added, snatching up a seventy-millimeter camera and lens in one hand and displaying it to Borman and Lovell. He gathered the brackets that would be attached to the windows to hold the cameras, then reappeared carrying it all heaped in his arms.

Borman watched him warily. Three men in so cramped a space reminded him of a crowd of monkeys in a small room, and any errant move could cause a switch to be bumped or a circuit to be broken without anyone noticing.

"Hey, look, just slow down. Take your time, okay?" he ordered.

Anders complied as best he could and spent the minutes until reacquisition of signal assembling his gear a bit more patiently. The twenty hours they'd be spending in lunar orbit would, he knew, go fast. And although Anders hadn't trained to be a photographer, it was the job he had been handed and he was determined to do it fully and well.

✳ ✳ ✳ ✳ ✳ ✳ ✳ ✳

When contact with the ground was at last reestablished and the Mission Controllers had finished their brief, noisy celebration, the capcom and the crew spent the time they had before the television show confirming the spacecraft's orbital coordinates and the status of the SPS. Anders then unpacked the TV camera and positioned it at the window, preparing to begin the live broadcast to the portion of the world that was awake.

This time, the camera's lens would not be pointed back at the indistinct blob of a planet that, the last time the TV audience had seen it, was 180,000 miles away and growing steadily smaller. Instead, it would be taking in the surface of the moon a scant five dozen miles below. By then the sun's angle was growing more acute, and Anders had installed a filter that would take advantage of that fact, meaning that the craters and rills and scarps and cliffs that were currently casting sharp shadows would be discernible even on television screens a quarter million miles away.

Once the broadcast from the ship began, the TV signal came first to the movie-theater-like viewing screen in Mission

Control. The spacecraft was at that point passing over the Sea of Fertility, the 522-mile-wide plain on the eastern limb of the moon formed by a vast lava bleed that resulted from a meteor hit four billion years earlier.

Almost as one, the TV producers signaled their networks to flick the switches that would spill the feed out to their broadcast centers and from there, to the world beyond. Jerry Carr knew that was his signal to start the show.

"*Apollo 8*, Houston," he called up, affecting a jauntiness that was clearly for the benefit of the television audience rather than the astronauts. "What does the ol' moon look like from sixty miles? Over."

"Okay, Houston, the moon is essentially gray, no color," Lovell answered. "Looks like plaster of paris or sort of a grayish deep sand. The Sea of Fertility doesn't stand out as well as it does back on Earth."

Lovell continued to narrate the features crawling past his window. After the Messier and Pickering craters came the Pyrenees Mountains, named after the snowy, far prettier range separating Spain from France. Then, as the ship sailed over the shore of the Sea of Tranquility, Lovell saw another landmark. The spot was significant to NASA because it might be used as an approach point for a later landing, but it mattered to Lovell for a more personal reason.

"We can see the second initial point," he said, "the Triangular Mountain."

The Triangular Mountain was the prosaic name NASA had assigned the potential approach point, but Lovell thought of it as Mount Marilyn. He had promised his wife that he would give it that name, and now he decided to call the formation that for the rest of the mission. It might be informal, and it might cause confusion among the NASA mapmakers, but the more Mount Marilyn got used on the air-to-ground loop, the likelier it was to stick.

The broadcast continued for a few minutes more, taking the crew—and by extension, the audience—over more craters. Lovell peered ahead to the shadowed portion of the moon, which lay well forward; squinting, he tried to see if, in the absence of sunlight, the darkened hemisphere that was approaching might be discernible in the faint light reflecting off the Earth and back to the moon.

"I can't see anything in earthshine at this present time," he said.

He used the word casually, familiarly, but to the viewers it was not remotely familiar. "Earthshine"—a word that had no meaning until today, until humans had gone to a place where earthshine existed and mattered. It was a wonderful notion, and one the television audience might have taken a moment to savor. But suddenly, seemingly with no warning, the feed from the moon cut out.

NASA had again scheduled the moment that the broadcast would stop, but again no one at the agency had thought to prepare a proper sign-off. There would be another broadcast, during the ship's ninth orbit, and perhaps something better could be planned for then.

After the show ended, Borman was relieved to be able to

get back to work. He was delighted with the job his main engine had performed, but it would be needed again for the Trans-Earth Injection—or TEI—burn during the blackout after the tenth revolution to get the spacecraft out of the moon's orbit and back on its way to Earth. NASA had promised to keep him apprised of the data readouts from the LOI burn to determine if there had been any hidden problems like the earlier helium bump.

Borman glanced over at Lovell and Anders, who were still allowing themselves a few more moments to sightsee.

"While these guys are looking at the moon, I want to make sure we have a good SPS," he told the capcom. "How about giving me that report when you can."

"Sure will, Frank," Carr replied.

Before the beginning of every revolution, or orbit, Borman would wait for an official okay from the ground that the spacecraft was fit. If he didn't get that assurance, Borman would assume that his ship was *not* fit, and he would fire his engine and aim for the home planet earlier than planned.

✳ ✳ ✳ ✳ ✳ ✳ ✳ ✳

Apollo 8 slipped back into lunar silence one hour and forty-eight minutes after it had emerged. The blackout would again be thirty-five minutes long, and when the crew reappeared and began the second revolution, there would be more landmark sightings to take, particularly of some of the other landing zones NASA was considering beyond the Sea of Tranquility.

There would also be craters to spot and name. There would

be craters named for the *Apollo 1* astronauts lost in the fire—Crater Grissom, Crater White and Crater Chaffee—and for other astronauts who had died before ever getting to space. There would be craters for Bob Gilruth, Chris Kraft and Jim Webb, NASA aristocracy. And, of course, there would be craters Borman, Lovell and Anders, far in the south lunar hemisphere.

Finally, some craters would be named on the fly. When they flew past a small formation, Anders declared, "We will call it John Aaron's," referring to a twenty-five-year-old Mission Control whiz who oversaw the spacecraft's environmental control systems and impressed nearly everyone who worked with him with his native smarts.

Aaron, sitting at his console, popped his head up and smiled—and Anders seemed almost to know it. "If he'll keep looking at our systems, anyway," the astronaut said.

"He just quit looking," Carr said with a wink at Aaron, who promptly went back to work.

✦ ✦ ✦ ✦ ✦ ✦ ✦ ✦

By the time the ship slipped into its fourth blackout, the astronauts were clearly exhausted. All three men had been awake throughout the entire final approach to the moon and the harrowing LOI burn. Now, with seven more revolutions to come and the TEI burn less than fifteen hours away, there was little chance that they would be able to relax and get some sleep before the homeward cruise.

Anders, perhaps more than all of them, had a very crowded

schedule. He was barely a quarter of the way through his photography checklist, and toward the end of the fourth blackout, he needed Borman to maneuver the ship so that he could bring the proper landmarks into focus.

Borman gripped his thruster handle and pitched the ship up slightly. The spacecraft was now positioned in such a way that for the first time, the astronauts could see all the way to the horizon of the moon, beyond which lay a huge swath of black sky. None of the men had thought about what that would mean—that when they came around the near side of the moon and once again established a straight line of radio communication between them and the Earth, they would also establish a straight line of sight. That, in turn, would allow for a view of their home planet rising above the bleak lunar plains.

"Oh my God!" Borman suddenly said. "Look at that picture over there! Here's the Earth coming up. Wow, is that pretty!"

The two other men looked out their windows. Just as Borman said, the blue-white ball that was home to everything they knew—home to every creature and thing and event that had occurred or existed across the entire expanse of Earth's history—was hovering over the pitted wreck that was the lunar landscape. The astronauts had seen the Earth and they had seen the moon, but this was the first time they had seen them together—the ugly, broken world beneath them and the lovely, breakable one in front of them.

It was Anders who shook himself from his reverie first, struggling to remove the black-and-white magazine from his camera and replace it with something that would better capture what he was seeing. "Hand me that roll of color, quick," he said to Lovell.

Anders took several shots. But only one of the images would matter. Only one, now hidden invisibly inside Anders's camera, would eventually move people to understand that worlds—like glass—do break and that the particular world in the photograph needed to be cared for more gently than humans ever had before. That was the picture—the one that would be called "Earthrise"— that rested inside Bill Anders's camera.

But on Christmas Eve day, 1968, nobody knew it.

THIRTEEN

Christmas Eve 1968

THE TELEVISION NETWORKS would get their billion people. They didn't think such a thing was possible—or at least not possible yet, not in 1968, when a billion-person audience would mean a third of the people on the planet stopping what they were doing to turn on a television set and watch the same broadcast at the same moment.

But the numbers coming into the networks said otherwise. It wasn't just North America and Western Europe that watched the first, poorly timed broadcast from *Apollo 8* in lunar orbit. It was all of Europe, on both sides of the East-West divide— including the grim, gray bunker that was East Berlin—with the nations in the Soviet orbit either parting the Iron Curtain to let the broadcast through or giving up the fight to keep the people who lived there from pirating the television signal. That first broadcast was watched in Central America and South America and Japan and South Korea and throughout much of the war zone that was Southeast Asia. It was watched in India and Africa and Australia. It was watched on American naval vessels and military bases around the world. It was watched more or less anywhere there were TV sets, electricity and human beings interested in tuning in to the first-ever broadcast from a different world.

"Your TV program was a big success," Mike Collins called up to the spacecraft late on Christmas Eve morning. "It was viewed by most of the nations of your neighboring planet, the Earth."

That audience would surely be dwarfed by the one for the evening broadcast that was still to come—the show that would air during the Western hemisphere's Christmas Eve, when people would be gathered with their families and friends and, in the American time zones at least, would have just had their dinners and sung their holiday songs and settled back on their sofas to hear what the men circling the moon had to say to them. The three astronauts would be on their ninth lunar revolution when they spoke, and after the tenth they would attempt to fire their engine again and return to Earth. If the engine worked, the broadcast would be remembered as a lyric celebration of a job brilliantly done. If it did not work, the broadcast would be known as an elegy, final words to mourn the dead.

The NASA image-makers may not have fully anticipated just how huge the viewership for the television show would be, but they suspected it would set records. Whatever the crew said, it had better be good.

✳ ✳ ✳ ✳ ✳ ✳ ✳ ✳

The day unspooled slowly in Houston—too slowly for the people of NASA who were involved in the mission, to say nothing of the much smaller group of people who lived with and loved the men flying it.

If the kids missed their dads or were at all worried, they kept their feelings to themselves and carried on. The older ones might escape for a few hours to the relative quiet of friends' homes that weren't packed with anxious, chattering, overexcited guests or surrounded by broadcast towers. In the Borman, Lovell and Anders households, the moms worked on as they had for much of the week, which meant taking care of the children and hosting the guests and satisfying the unceasing needs of the media. Susan Borman had slept little and felt ragged.

Valerie Anders remained indoors with her children and came outside to talk whenever the press needed a statement; the rest of the time, the reporters saw little of her. Like Susan Borman and Marilyn Lovell, she knew how critical the LOI burn was, and she had stayed awake for it. But she passed those crucial minutes in her own way, surrounded by a tight clutch of friends, listening to the squawk box in her darkened living room, with the Christmas tree and the fireplace providing the only illumination.

When Valerie stepped outside to address the reporters after learning that the burn had been successful, she did so with a polish suited more to a senator than to the young wife of a hero.

"The significance of historical events cannot be realized immediately," she said, "nor can the impact or magnitude of the event be adequately described at the time of the occurrence. Though history is being made today, we all need to try and comprehend the years of effort by many people involved in the eventual lunar landing."

The reporters raced to take it all down. Valerie, her job complete, went back inside to make sure her five small children hadn't wrecked the house in the few short moments she had been gone.

Marilyn Lovell—the most experienced of the three wives and indeed the most experienced astronaut wife in the world, measured by the amount of time her husband had spent in space—knew she would have to make time for a nap, and she did so, too, just as soon as the LOI burn was done and the first broadcast had signed off. She also knew that if she could possibly manage it, she needed a few minutes out of the house.

Christmas week had always meant church for her and her family, and they had found a comfortable episcopal congregation in Houston with a popular minister—Father Donald Raish— who knew all the Lovells well. Attending a proper Christmas Eve service today would be impossible, what with the business of getting the children ready and navigating the media storm that would erupt the moment the entire family emerged on the front lawn.

Instead, Marilyn called Father Raish and asked if she might come by early, perhaps to have a private moment inside the church. He agreed, and late in the afternoon she left the house alone, fielded as few questions from the press as she could, hopped in her car and drove to the church.

When she arrived and went inside, she could see that the sanctuary was almost empty, save for Father Raish and the organist. Candles were lit, the organ was playing and Father Raish greeted her. They walked to the altar and Marilyn prayed. She was happy for the quiet moment and grateful for the effort that had been made on her behalf.

"You did all this for me?" she asked Father Raish.

"Well, you have to miss mass tonight, so yes," he answered modestly.

Marilyn smiled, thanked him and hurried back out to her car. It was already getting dark. As she approached her home, the trees above the road appeared to part: directly in front of her the moon hung in the sky. She stopped the car and looked up at it.

Jim is up there, she thought.

Marilyn sat with that idea for a moment, then drove the rest of the way to her brightly lit and very crowded home. The nighttime broadcast was still hours away, and the house would only get brighter and more crowded still.

✳ ✳ ✳ ✳ ✳ ✳ ✳ ✳

Of the three men circling the moon in the small *Apollo* spacecraft, Borman was the only one who would admit that he was flat-out exhausted. Lovell seemed tireless, but then, he was never as happy as when he was in space. Anders, meantime, could not sit still. He was five years younger than Borman and Lovell, but the way he bounced from window to window taking his sightings and snapping his pictures put Borman in mind of his boys when they were in grade school.

In truth, however, both Anders and Lovell were wrung out; Borman could see it in the red that rimmed their eyes and the periodic yawns they tried to stifle. What's more, while Lovell would sometimes boast, with justification, about how deftly he could play the computer's keypad—"like a concert pianist," he liked to say—he couldn't hide his mistakes. Mostly the computer was silent, but if Lovell entered an erroneous command, the system would emit a warning tone. Borman had heard a few too many of those alerts, another sign that fatigue was taking a toll.

Mission rules allowed all three astronauts to schedule their sleep interval for the same time, but Borman preferred it if one of them kept watch.

"I'm going to sack out for an hour," he told Lovell and Anders. "One of you should, too."

Lovell, in the equipment bay, nodded vaguely. Anders held up a hand in a just-a-minute gesture.

Borman did not care to pull rank—not yet, anyway—but he could at least set a good example. He floated down to the equipment bay, rigged his sleeping bag and floated back out to confirm that his ship was in order. After deciding that it was, he drifted back down to the equipment bay.

Moments later, Anders and Lovell could hear Borman breathing steadily. For the next hour, Lovell worked with Anders to help him get caught up on his photography. Lovell—whose formal title was command-module pilot and who had both the ability and the authority to take the wheel of the ship whenever necessary—maneuvered the spacecraft to give Anders the angles he needed. Anders changed windows as required, working to get the alignment for each picture right.

Toward the end of the hour, the two men began struggling with a particularly difficult target.

"Ahhh!" Lovell exclaimed.

"What happened?" Anders asked.

"It's okay," Lovell reassured him.

"Don't wake up Frank."

But it was too late; Borman was awake. The motion of the ship and the ongoing background chatter had proven too much. He drifted out of his sleeping bag, rubbed his eyes and looked around him.

"Sorry Frank, didn't mean to disturb you," Lovell said.

Borman waved it off. The hour of sleep had helped; though he didn't feel anything like fully rested, he did feel much improved. Looking at his crewmen, however, he could see that the same hour hadn't done them any favors; the fatigue showing in their faces was becoming ever more evident. He would give them a little more time, through the remainder of the seventh rev, and then, whether they liked it or not, they'd go belowdecks, climb into their sleeping bags and, as they put it at West Point, go "local horizontal."

Lovell didn't need any persuading. He was more than willing to submit to Borman's authority at this moment. Anders hesitated, and Borman practically barked at him. "Right now! Go to bed! I'm not kidding you." After that, Anders finally relented and went to sleep, too.

Borman settled back into his left-hand seat. "Lovell's snoring already," he radioed quietly to the ground.

"Yes," Collins answered, "we can hear him down here."

✳ ✳ ✳ ✳ ✳ ✳ ✳ ✳

As the time for the Christmas Eve television show approached, Borman, Lovell and Anders were flying over the far side of the moon. Walter Cronkite went live from his studio in New York.

"*Apollo 8* is in its ninth and next-to-last full orbit of the moon," he began. "The astronauts, on the orders of command pilot Frank Borman, are scrubbing all remaining items from their flight plan except one more television transmission, which should come up very shortly now, because they are tired and need to rest before the critical maneuver that starts them back to Earth early tomorrow morning."

Cronkite went on. "We're all anxiously looking forward to this second set of pictures of the moon from seventy miles high and the spacecraft moving across the moon's surface at three thousand six hundred miles per hour." Numbers and names, the anchorman knew, were a good way to add substance to any part of a broadcast that was really just an exercise in filling time. "The person you'll be hearing speaking to *Apollo 8* is astronaut Ken Mattingly, who is so-called capcom, capsule communicator."

Finally, a voice and picture link was established. The screens in Mission Control, the New York studios and a billion homes around the world were once again filled with the moon.

"How's the TV look, Houston?" Anders asked.

"Loud and clear," Mattingly answered.

"It looks okay?"

"Very good."

Satisfied, Borman began. "This is *Apollo 8*, coming to you live from the moon," he said. His voice, traveling across a quarter million miles of void, sounded thinner and more nasal than it really was. But it was steady and strong, and so was the signal that carried it. "Bill Anders, Jim Lovell and myself have spent the day before Christmas doing experiments, taking pictures and firing our spacecraft engines to maneuver around. What we will do now is follow the trail we've been following all day and take you on through a lunar sunset."

The static crackled, but the picture stayed true, and Borman went on, following the narrative the crew had planned. "The moon is a different thing to each one of us," he said. "I know my own impression is that it's a vast, lonely, forbidding-type existence or expanse of nothing. It looks like clouds and clouds of pumice stone, and certainly not a very inviting place to live or work. Jim, what have you thought most about?"

"My thoughts are very similar," Lovell said. "The vast loneliness up here of the moon is awe-inspiring, and it makes you realize just what you have back there on Earth. The Earth from here is a grand oasis in the big vastness of space."

"Bill, what do you think?" Borman asked.

"I think the one thing that impressed me most was the lunar sunrises and sunsets," said Anders, still very much the photographer. "These in particular bring out the stark nature of the terrain, and the long shadows really bring out the relief that is hard to see at this very bright surface that we're going over now."

They were trying, these pilots who had been asked to play poets, and they were performing reasonably well. But it was Anders, staying true to what he was—a professional on a mission—who sounded the most authentic, and Borman and Lovell knew it. So for the rest of the broadcast, they made an unspoken decision to play it straight and simply narrate what they were seeing.

"The horizon here is very, very stark," Anders said. "The sky is pitch-black and the Earth"—Anders caught himself—"or the moon, rather, excuse me, is quite light."

The audience encountered the Marsh of Sleep again, and the Seas of Tranquility, Fertility and Crises. And then, finally, the ship approached what is known, too ominously, as the lunar terminator—the clean, sharp line on the airless moon where daylight instantly gives way to nighttime, with none of the luminous wash of sun through atmosphere that makes dawn and dusk so gradual on Earth. The thing about the terminator, though, is that it can be two things, either the dying of the light or the arrival of it, depending on whether you stand in the shadow and look at the sun or stand in the sun and look at the shadow. Borman knew which one he preferred.

"Now you can see the long shadows of the lunar sunrise," he said of what was actually a sunset, "and for all the people back on Earth, the crew of *Apollo 8* has a message we would like to send you."

Anders picked up the flight plan and turned to the last

page. Poetry might be alien to the three men, but at last they had verse to speak.

"'In the beginning,'" Anders began, "'God created the heaven and the Earth. And the Earth was without form and void, and darkness was upon the face of the deep; and the spirit of God moved upon the face of the waters. And God said, "Let there be light," and there was light.'"

Anders read a bit more and then Lovell picked up the words. "'And God called the light Day and the darkness He called Night. And the evening and the morning were the first day. And God said, "Let there be a firmament in the midst of the waters. And let it divide the waters from the waters."'"

Finally, when Lovell was through, Borman finished up. He read the ancient passage about the gathering of the waters, the appearance of the dry land, and the naming of the land and the waters, concluding with the words, "'And God saw that it was good.'" Then the commander of the crew that had ventured so far and seen so much spoke to the billion or so people who represented the entire questing species for whom they had made their journey.

"And from the crew of *Apollo 8*, we close with good night, good luck, a merry Christmas, and God bless all of you, all of you on the good Earth."

Then the signal from the spacecraft cut off and the men circling the moon were once again alone, beings apart. Now, with the broadcast over, it would be up to the men and women and children on the home planet to make what they would of the images they had just seen and the words they had just heard.

* * * * * * * *

Frank Borman, finished with the television broadcast, was still in command of an active spacecraft, and that spacecraft was still locked in a repeating orbit around the moon. Once the TV show was over, he was eager to get back to the business at hand.

On the ground, many of the controllers were not quite ready to let go of the feelings they had just experienced. The scientific cathedral of Mission Control had, if only briefly, become a spiritual one.

So Borman waited until he was reasonably sure the broadcast had ended and then waited a beat longer. Sensing the power of the moment that had just passed, he wanted to make certain that his next words would get through to Mission Control, but not go beyond.

"Are we off the air now?" he asked.

"That's affirmative, *Apollo 8*, you are," Ken Mattingly answered evenly.

"Did you read everything we had to say there?"

"Loud and clear. Thank you for a real good show."

"Okay. Now, Ken, we'd like to get squared away for TEI here," Borman said. "Can you give us some good words like you promised?"

"Yes, sir," Mattingly answered.

The good words Borman wanted were the computer commands for the return-to-Earth burn, as well as other details like the navigational star sightings Lovell would need to take and the precise length of the burn.

Borman was well aware of the importance of these kinds of calculations. During the broadcast, he may have sounded nonchalant when speaking about how the crew had been "firing our spacecraft engines to maneuver around," but that glossed over the fact that "maneuvering around" took a lot of planning and a lot of fuel. Good words from Ken Mattingly would go a long way toward minimizing the attendant risk when you're aiming to place a spacecraft in a very narrow reentry target in the Earth's atmosphere 233,000 miles away.

Mattingly spent a fair bit of the ninth revolution sending up the necessary alignments and other settings. Borman and Anders copied it all out in longhand, like operators at telegraph keys. Lovell, at his computer, punched in the coordinates.

"Basically," Mattingly concluded when he was at last done, "all systems are good. After one hundred thirty-eight seconds of the burn, you are on your way home. The weather in the recovery area looks good."

Borman acknowledged Mattingly's report but made no response to the capcom's mention of the recovery area. Weather could change well before *Apollo 8* returned to Earth, and certainly the fortunes of the spacecraft could, too. For now, the crew was headed toward the end of their ninth orbit and their second-to-last thirty-five minutes of blackout.

"Thanks a lot," Borman said without ceremony. "We'll see you around the next pass."

✷ ✷ ✷ ✷ ✷ ✷ ✷ ✷

As the hour of the Trans-Earth Injection burn approached, Susan Borman decided she would handle *Apollo 8*'s final burn differently from the way she'd handled the Lunar Orbit Insertion. She still preferred to keep the press and most of the guests in her home at a safe remove during the mission's most critical moments, but the solitary vigil she had maintained for the LOI burn had also left her spent. This time around, she decided to share the high-wire wait with at least one other person by her side, and she very much wanted that person to be Valerie Anders. Valerie lived just a few lawns and a short stroll away. Marilyn lived much farther away, which would require her to get in her car and drive through the mobs of press in order to get to the Bormans' home. So Susan had invited Valerie to drop by for the Christmas Eve broadcast and the engine burn, and Valerie had accepted. Before long, the two women slipped away from the crowd of well-wishers in the living room, repaired to the kitchen nook and began their vigil.

Marilyn chose not to change a thing: she would follow the coverage in her home just as she had all the other critical moments in the mission, with her friends and family grouped around her, in front of the TV. After the crew's broadcast but before the burn, she and her children had gone for a walk. The nearby houses were always decorated during the holiday season, but this evening Marilyn and the kids were surprised to see that almost all her neighbors had gone further than usual and lined the sidewalks with homemade luminaries. Up and down the street, carefully positioned candles flickered inside paper bags in tribute to the men aboard *Apollo 8*. Maybe, fifteen-year-old

Barbara Lovell imagined, her dad would be able to see the glow from space and know that they were all rooting for the crew.

Marilyn could not personally thank every one of her neighbors, but she could express her appreciation for the attention her family had been shown all week in another way. After she got home and put the children to bed, she went into her kitchen, arranged cups of eggnog on a large tray and went back to the front lawn to pass the Christmas cheer out to the press, who were very far from their own homes tonight. Then she went back inside and gathered with her guests in front of the TV.

Walter Cronkite framed the stakes for the TEI burn in a stark way.

"While *Apollo 8* is behind the moon out of touch with the ground control again, the astronauts are to start up that big rocket engine that powered them into lunar orbit," he said. "It must work perfectly again because if it fails, *Apollo 8* could be caught in that lunar orbit. That, of course, is not expected to happen. The engine has worked perfectly so far. It should work once more."

That was true as far as it went, but it didn't go far. As the astronauts, their families and everyone at NASA knew very well, completely reliable systems worked only until the moment they became completely unreliable.

✳ ✳ ✳ ✳ ✳ ✳ ✳

Shortly before the blackout at the end of the tenth orbit, Ken Mattingly made the call that began the countdown to the final burn that was designed to bring the astronauts home.

"Okay, *Apollo 8*," he said. "We've reviewed all your systems. You have a go for TEI."

"Okay," Borman answered.

As the clock ticked toward what everyone hoped would be the final loss of signal, Mattingly began the ritual of calling off the time.

"*Apollo 8*, Houston. We have three minutes to LOS. All systems are go."

There was no answer from the ship.

"*Apollo 8*, *Apollo 8*, this is Houston," Mattingly repeated. "Three minutes LOS. All systems are go. Over."

"Roger, thank you, Houston. *Apollo 8*," Borman responded with a clear emphasis on the last two words. There was a conclusory note to the sign-off, one that did not invite further chatter unless it was necessary.

Mattingly, fluent in the commander's tongue, held his own for the next three minutes. For the only time in the mission thus far, there would be no steady countdown to a pivotal event.

Finally, just seconds before blackout, the capcom sent up an all-business good-bye.

"All systems are go, *Apollo 8*."

"Thank you," Borman answered.

Then the line went dead.

✳ ✳ ✳ ✳ ✳ ✳ ✳ ✳

Inside the spacecraft, the astronauts took a moment to sit quietly. It was a relief to be freed from the stream of must-do chores that were forever being read off to them. Then they went about making the final preparations for the TEI burn as wordlessly as they could—saying what they had to, avoiding anything else.

When the burn was less than thirty minutes away, Borman finally spoke up again.

"It's been a pretty fantastic week, hasn't it?" he said.

Lovell smiled, thinking of home. "It's going to get better," he said.

For the next twenty minutes, they worked on various routine tasks. Anders glanced out his window. "Boy, it's blacker than pitch out there," he said.

Borman looked at his clock, which indicated the time remaining until the burn. "Seven minutes," he said. "Coming up on six minutes."

As they had before, the astronauts settled back into their couches and loosely fastened their seat restraints. They were about to experience a lot of acceleration in just over two minutes. Once again, the crew would be pushed back in their seats with a comparatively gentle hand of less than one g, though after four days of no g's at all, it would feel like a lot more.

"Stand by for two minutes," Anders said.

After the final seconds ticked down, the computer flashed its 99:20 last-chance code.

Lovell reached forward and pressed PROCEED.

✴ ✴ ✴ ✴ ✴ ✴ ✴

The atmosphere in Mission Control wasn't at all what Chris Kraft wanted it to be. His controllers were professionals and they generally abided by the rules of the room, which meant concentrating on the work and keeping extraneous talk to a minimum. But those rules were usually relaxed during blackouts, whether they were the new lunar variety or the more familiar ones of a *Gemini* or *Mercury* ship briefly vanishing between tracking stations. During those intervals, with the headsets silent and the telemetry shooting blanks, no one objected if a man exchanged a few words with the fellow to his left or right.

This blackout, however, was different. In less than twenty minutes, Mission Control would get either very good news or very bad news, depending on what the SPS did. If the news was bad, it would likely mean the loss of three good men. Kraft now knew, as he hadn't known twenty-three months before, what losing three men felt like, and he never wanted to experience such a thing again. So although the room was reasonably quiet, under the circumstances it was not as quiet as Kraft felt it should be.

"Could you please shut up?" Kraft growled. "I don't know about the rest of you, but I'm thinking about whether these guys are going to come out the other side."

Kraft scanned the room and darkened his look to make it clear that the scolding was for everyone.

Back at the astronauts' homes, nobody had to ask for silence. Susan Borman and Valerie Anders were seated side by side, alone, in the Bormans' kitchen nook. Marilyn sat on her living room floor with her knees tucked up, just as she had during the television broadcast hours earlier.

On the bottom of the TV screens tuned to the coverage of *Apollo 8* and at the top of the main screen in Mission Control, the mission's elapsed time ticked up to three days, seventeen hours, nineteen minutes and twelve seconds. Some of the viewers at home might have known without being told that this was the moment the burn was supposed to begin. Every single person in Mission Control knew it well. If the engine lit as planned, it would speed the ship to an early exit from its final blackout, and the crew would regain radio contact just fifteen minutes and ten seconds later.

The engine burn—invisibly, unknowably—either would or wouldn't take place, and the long wait for news from the ship would pass the way Kraft had wanted it to, in silence. Instead, fingers were drummed and throats were cleared and the mission clock counted off the time.

A bit less than twelve minutes after the burn should have happened, Mattingly made his first call. As with the LOI burn, it was too soon to expect reacquisition of signal, but not too soon to begin hoping for it.

"*Apollo 8*, Houston," Mattingly said to the invisible spacecraft and, by extension, to the global television audience.

He was met by silence.

"*Apollo 8*, Houston," he repeated eighteen seconds later.

Again nothing—only the loud hiss of cosmic absence in his headset and on the TVs.

He tried again after twenty-eight more seconds. "*Apollo 8*, Houston."

This time, hearing nothing, he gave it nearly a minute. His next call received no response, either.

After letting another forty-eight seconds pass, Mattingly hailed the ship yet again.

More silence. Now the fifteen minutes and ten seconds were well and truly gone. If the spacecraft did not appear soon, it would be seriously overdue.

And then, as one, the dead screens at every console in front of every man in Mission Control began to jump and flicker. All at once they were filled with numbers—beautifully complete and beautifully healthy numbers—streaming to them from a spacecraft that was still a quarter million miles away but was undeniably speeding its way home.

A moment later, Jim Lovell's voice came through clearly.

"Houston, *Apollo 8*," he said. "Please be informed there is a Santa Claus."

"That's affirmative," Mattingly responded. "You are the best ones to know."

That, at least, is what the astronauts heard. But the people in Mission Control did not, because the capcom's words were drowned out by the whooping and cheering and whistling from the controllers who now didn't give a fig for Chris Kraft's rule of silence.

In the Bormans' kitchen nook, Susan leapt up, waved her hands excitedly in the air and then brought them down to take Valerie in a happy hug. In the Lovell home, Marilyn stood at the center of a similarly raucous scene, and the noisy crowd soon woke the children she had just put to bed.

There was much applause, too, in homes and in bars and on American military bases around the world. Also celebrating the moment were the 1,700 men aboard the aircraft carrier USS *Yorktown*, the prime recovery vessel, which was already steaming into position in the South Pacific for the splashdown that was now just over two days away.

From the spacecraft, which still had a long way to go before it landed in that small spot of ocean, Frank Borman had only one question.

"What's next on the docket?" he asked.

FOURTEEN

December 25–27, 1968

DEKE SLAYTON WAS well aware that communications protocols frowned upon anyone but the capcom—even the head of the astronaut office—talking to the crews, but after the TEI burn he felt like making an exception.

"Good morning, *Apollo 8*. Deke here," he said, after plugging his headset into a second jack at the capcom station. "I just would like to wish you a very merry Christmas on behalf of everyone in the control center and I'm sure everyone around the world."

Slayton getting even a little sappy was not something the crew had ever experienced before, and they did not know quite how to respond. That mattered little, however, because apparently a sappy Slayton was also a chatty Slayton.

"None of us ever expected to have a better Christmas present than this one. Hope you get a good night's sleep from here on and enjoy your Christmas dinner tomorrow. We look forward to seeing you in Hawaii on the twenty-eighth."

Borman waited till he was sure Slayton was done and only then responded. "Okay, leader," he began, an unexpectedly deferential form of address and one he hadn't used before. But the commander of the mission was not entirely immune to sentiment, either. "We'll see you there," he said. "Thank everyone on the ground for us. It's pretty clear we wouldn't be anywhere if we didn't have them helping us out."

"We concur that," Slayton said.

"Even Mr. Kraft does something right once in a while," Anders added.

Slayton glanced over his shoulder to see if Kraft took the ship-to-shore sass in good humor. But Kraft wasn't in the room: with the spacecraft at last on its way to Earth, he had run home for a nap and a change of clothes.

"He got tired of waiting for you to talk and went home," Slayton answered.

As Slayton hoped they would, the astronauts did get some sleep—Borman and Lovell first and then Anders when they awoke. And they did have their Christmas dinner, later in the day on Christmas proper.

Like all the other meals they'd had so far, these were wrapped and stacked in a bin in the equipment bay. But the Christmas dinner packages were heavier than usual, and each was wrapped in green fireproof ribbon with a card reading MERRY CHRISTMAS. When the astronauts took off the outer wrapping, they discovered that the plastic pouches contained turkey and gravy and cranberry sauce and stuffing. All three astronauts smiled at the meal, which, after four days of flight rations, looked like a feast.

Not long after they ate, Lovell radioed down to the ground. "It appears we did a grave injustice to the food people," he said. "Santa Claus brought us a TV dinner each, which was delicious: turkey and gravy, cranberry sauce, grape punch. Outstanding."

Milt Windler, at the flight director's station, laughed. In front of him, on a clear spot on the console's little desk area, was a cup of coffee and a baloney sandwich resting on a crinkled piece of wax paper. Just this once, the men in space were eating better than the men on the ground.

＊＊＊＊＊＊＊＊

The Apollo 8 families spent Christmas Day in a more traditional way. Valerie Anders gathered up her five children and drove to nearby Ellington Air Force Base, where they attended Catholic services at the base chapel. Susan Borman, accompanied by her boys and her parents-in-law, drove to St. Christopher's Episcopal Church, where the Reverend James Buckner read a prayer particular to the most conspicuous member of the congregation, who could not be in attendance that day:

"O, eternal God in whose domain are all the planets, stars and galaxies and all the reaches of time and space, from infinity to infinity," he said, "watch over and protect, we pray, the astronauts of our country."

The Christmas Eve broadcast had caught some of the kids by surprise. Fred hadn't expected his father to recite verse the night before because the astronauts were usually laser-focused on the technical details and minutiae of the mission. Tonight things were different and Fred found it heartening that they took a few moments to invoke scripture and express the magnitude of the mission. And here was Reverend Buckner, beaming some of those celestial blessings back up to the spacecraft.

Marilyn Lovell's Christmas morning began with an act of charity. Almost everyone in the media crowd who had filled her lawn for most of the week had briefly decamped to celebrate the day, and now there was just one photographer left. Marilyn peeked out her window and took pity on the man.

"Why don't you go home?" she asked, standing on the front step with her arms folded against the chill. "We're not coming out now."

"I can't go home," the man said forlornly.

"Why not?" Marilyn asked.

"I can't leave until I get a picture."

Marilyn laughed. "Is that all?" she said.

Looking over her shoulder into the living room, she saw that her youngest, Jeffrey, and her oldest, Barbara, were sitting by the Christmas tree amid the morning's presents.

"Kids!" she called. "Come over here." Both children jumped up, but they were empty-handed. "No, no," she said, gesturing toward the mound of gifts, "bring something."

Barbara collected whatever toy was in reach, Jeffrey grabbed a pogo stick that he'd been trying to master for much of the morning, and they both went outside. Jeffrey bounced while Barbara posed and the reporter took a few pictures. Then he hurried off to spend a few hours of Christmas Day on his own time.

Not long afterward, Marilyn's holiday generosity was repaid. Unannounced, a Rolls-Royce pulled up to the curb and a uniformed man climbed out. He came up the walk, knocked on the door and presented Marilyn with a box from the Neiman Marcus department store. It was wrapped in sky-blue paper and decorated with two Styrofoam balls—one larger, one smaller; one painted like the Earth, one painted like the moon. Attached was a note that read, "Merry Christmas. With love from the man in the moon." Inside was a mink jacket.

Marilyn Lovell, wife of the moon man, wore her gift to church with her children by her side that morning. And if it looked to anyone in the Houston community like she was putting on airs, well, so be it. She had done more than enough this week to earn the indulgence.

✳ ✳ ✳ ✳ ✳ ✳ ✳ ✳

By late Christmas Day, a lot of people, including some in the media, began to believe that the Apollo 8 mission was effectively over. Yes, the crew still had to land their spacecraft, but that was really just a formality, wasn't it? Commentators on television had begun offering guesses about which cities would host parades and where the astronauts would go on the world tour that would follow. But Borman demanded vigilance.

Apollo 8's flight back to the home planet might appear to be the equivalent of long-distance skydiving, but as with skydiving, it could still go badly awry. In the hours since the TEI, in fact, the mission had nearly come undone, though the news was little reported on Earth.

Borman had been sleeping off his Christmas dinner in the

equipment bay while Anders minded the ship in the left-hand couch and Lovell worked the computer. Collins was reading him new coordinates for the rotisserie roll that kept the spacecraft evenly heated on all sides. Now and then, the positioning of the ship had to be changed depending on its ever-shifting angle relative to the sun. Lovell was punching the commands into the computer when suddenly the thrusters began firing. The spacecraft swayed dizzyingly, causing it to swing from its roughly nose-forward position to a straight nose-up attitude.

"Whoa, whoa, whoa!" Lovell exclaimed.

"Okay, whoa, whoa. Standing by," Collins responded.

Anders watched as the positioning indicator on the instrument panel swung in parallel to the ship; Borman awoke with a start.

"What happened?" he demanded.

For the moment, Lovell didn't have an answer and the spacecraft continued to lurch. Anders fired the thrusters to return the ship to its proper orientation, but whatever bit of bad code had initiated the problem was fighting back, working to maintain the nose-up position. Knowing that the first rule for this kind of situation was to avoid introducing new problems when one is already unfolding, Anders let go of the thruster handle.

Lovell ran his computer commands in his head and quickly figured out what he had done. Collins had called up a verb 3723 and a noun 501, which would have positioned the ship in the proper roll angle. Lovell, his fatigue getting the better of him, had inadvertently shortened it to verb 37 and noun 01. Those were very different commands: "verb 37" meant "Return to

Earth," and "01" meant "Prelaunch Mode." In effect, Lovell had told the spacecraft it was on the launchpad in Florida, and the spacecraft believed him—hence its proud nose-up position as it prepared for liftoff.

"It was my goof," Lovell said.

Collins, who had already correctly guessed what the cause of the problem was, answered simply, "Roger."

The scrambled coding could be fixed, but it would take some work. Due to the incorrect commands, the spacecraft's brain had been wiped clean of any knowledge of its current orientation.

Lovell was able to restore the alignment in comparatively short order. When he was finished, he reflected that it was a good procedure for any *Apollo* commander to have in his back pocket. In the event that a future spacecraft ever suffered a catastrophic systems failure, the first thing he'd need to know is how to get the ship pointed properly again.

✳ ✳ ✳ ✳ ✳ ✳ ✳

Avoidable errors like Lovell's were nothing compared to the unavoidable hazards that still awaited the spacecraft during reentry. The first critical step would come less than an hour before the ship made its initial contact with the atmosphere, when it would jettison the service module with its engine and long-term life-support systems. The spacecraft that began its journey at the top of a 363-foot stack of rocket would then be reduced to an eleven-foot-tall cone with a heat shield covering its blunt bottom and enough oxygen and power to keep the crew alive for just a few hours.

That capsule would collide with the atmosphere at nearly 25,000 miles per hour, and withstanding that high-velocity hammer blow would be only part of the challenge. The spacecraft would also have to thread its way into a fifteen-mile-wide keyhole in the sky, which is an exceedingly small target if you're taking a bead on it from a quarter million miles away. On a far smaller scale, one in which the Earth is the size of a basketball and the moon is the size of a baseball, the two worlds would be positioned fourteen feet apart and the fifteen-mile reentry corridor would be no thicker than a piece of paper.

The consequences of missing that target would be immediate. Come in too steep and the crew would be killed by the g-forces, assuming the spacecraft didn't come apart from the aerodynamic violence first. Come in too shallow and *Apollo 8* would skip off the skin of the atmosphere and bounce into the void forever. Even a successful reentry would require riding the fire to splashdown in a way no crew had ever done before, with the temperature on the heat shield climbing to 5,000 degrees Fahrenheit—or twice the melting point of steel—compared to the 3,000 degrees of orbital reentry. The intense heat would cause the spacecraft to be surrounded by a cloud of ionized gas that would be impenetrable to radio signals, meaning that this life-or-death maneuver, like so many others on this mission, would take place during a blackout.

There was still more to worry about. Assuming the crew could hit the ballistic bull's-eye, the reentry would still not be survivable if the spacecraft didn't do some complex back-and-forth maneuvering on the way down to keep the intense heat and gravitational pressure from killing them. The physics of this so-called skip reentry were not unlike those of a roller coaster: the first plunge is always the steepest, and each successive peak and valley is lower and shallower, as the gravitational energy that is accumulated during the slow, clanking climb to the top of the ride's first peak is steadily dissipated.

The skip reentry would be a wild ride, and it would have been awfully nice to have test-flown the flight path from just a few thousand miles above Earth once or twice before. But since this was the first time any human had tried to head home from the moon, the astronauts' test flight would be a real flight from a true lunar distance.

And that's why Frank Borman did not care a whit for talk of parades and world tours.

✷ ✷ ✷ ✷ ✷ ✷ ✷ ✷

It was deep in the Pacific night when the spacecraft from the moon was making its final approach to Earth. If you lived on one of the islands in the middle of the ocean, you could have seen the ship coming, which by then would look like a tiny dot of light and would be just over sixty minutes from entering the Earth's atmosphere, moving at about 20,000 miles per hour and still accelerating.

Aboard the dot, the experience was very different and much less peaceful. The men in the machine couldn't feel the ship's motion, but the Earth, which had been as small as a coin just two days before, was growing fast, expanding well beyond the frames of the spacecraft's windows and once again becoming an enormous arc of horizon that was far too big to be seen whole in a single field. From the distance of the moon, Jim Lovell had marveled that he could extend his arm and hide the entire Earth behind his thumb. Now, as the planet resumed its proper scale, his thumb was once again a near nothing against the great mass of the world.

Before the crew could fly much closer to that growing bulk, they had a lot to do. As soon as reentry caused even a ghost of gravity to appear, any loose debris that had been floating around the cockpit would fall down to the base of the spacecraft, which meant onto the astronauts. This problem would only get worse as the g-forces grew: you do not want to get hit in the head by a seven-g flashlight or bolt when you're trying to pilot a spacecraft through free fall.

Borman and Lovell did a fast cleanup of the spacecraft. Anders, meanwhile, made sure the valves on the potable water tank and any coolant systems or evaporators were closed, since water raining down on the electronics would be even worse than junk raining down on the crew. Lovell watched Anders to ensure that the job got done and then called the ground to confirm.

"Bill just shut the potable inlet, Ken," he radioed to Mattingly.

"Okay, thank you."

"If I see any water floating around, I'll give you another call," Anders added.

The comment was meant to reassure, but it did no such thing. By now, any loose water that hadn't shown itself probably wouldn't appear until it came out of hiding during reentry, and then it would be too late.

Anders also had to adjust the environmental control system so that the cabin temperature fell to 62 degrees, though that chill wouldn't last long. Even the best-insulated ship would experience some heat soak when its leading edge was reaching 5,000 degrees. And by the time the fiery reentry was over, the ship would have traded the deep freeze of space for the 80-degree weather of the South Pacific, at which point it might grow uncomfortably warm inside.

Finally, the time came for the no-turning-back maneuver—the junking of the service module. Like so much else during this voyage, it would be an exercise in controlled violence, with explosive bolts blowing all links between the two parts of the ship.

"Houston, *Apollo 8*, confirm go for pyro arm," Lovell called down, asking for official clearance to arm the pyrotechnics that would effectively pull the pin on the jettison grenade.

"*Apollo 8*, you are go for pyro arm," Mattingly answered.

With that clearance from the ground, the astronauts returned to their seats and cinched their restraints as tight as possible. The loose settings used during the LOI and TEI burns would be nowhere near sufficient for the ride that lay ahead. After Borman belted himself in, he looked to Lovell and Anders to make sure they had done so as well. Then he looked at the clock on his instrument panel. The moment the service module was gone, he and his crew would be entering the period of peak risk. Within the hour, they would be safely in the water—or they would be casualties of space.

✶ ✶ ✶ ✶ ✶ ✶ ✶ ✶

In his center seat, Lovell tapped the commands that would initiate the separation sequence into the computer. After thinking for a moment, the computer processed what it had been told and flashed back the 99:20 go or no-go code.

"Go to proceed," Lovell called out.

"Go to proceed," Borman agreed. He placed his hand on his thruster controller in the event the maneuver went awry and the ship flew off course.

Lovell pressed the PROCEED key. As the bolts exploded, a dull thump, accompanied by a jolt, shook the astronauts. The command module popped free and the service module—drifting somewhere invisibly behind—fired the proper burst through its forward-facing thrusters and backed safely away.

Borman eyeballed his positioning indicators and relaxed his hand. His ship was stable.

"*That* was a kick," he said. Though he was fully aware of the power of the pyros, he was surprised that he had felt so much of the explosion's force.

Mission Control could see from its telemetry that the jettison had occurred, and Anders and Lovell had felt it as powerfully as Borman had. As a consequence, no one thought to say it aloud.

Reentry was now an inevitability, less than twelve minutes

away. But the success of that imminent collision between space-craft and air required one more navigational sighting.

Precisely six minutes before reentry began, the moon—remote once more—would rise over the horizon of the Earth, the last time the crew would see it through the void of space. If it showed itself at the expected moment, it would mean *Apollo 8*'s trajectory was true. If not, Lovell and Borman would have some fast and complicated navigating and flying to do to put their course right before time ran out.

Two minutes before the lunar sighting was due to occur, Anders, following the flight plan, called out, "Horizon check."

Lovell, who had been watching Borman from his adjacent seat, responded: "He's doing that now."

After some last-minute maneuvering, Borman looked through his window and smiled. "And look who's coming there, would you?"

"Yes!" Anders exclaimed, glancing ahead.

"You see it?"

"Yes."

"Just like they promised."

"What?" asked Lovell, who had been minding his instruments.

"The moon," Borman and Anders said in unison.

Lovell looked up and saw it, too—a tiny world that, like the Earth a few days ago, could fit behind his thumb.

"At six minutes before," Borman said, glancing at the flight plan, "just like it says."

Paul Haney, the NASA Mission Control commentator

currently on duty narrating events for broadcast now described for the television audience the coming sequence of events.

"The four-hundred-thousand-foot point is where they will begin to encounter some little bit of atmosphere," he said. "The blackout should begin some twenty-five seconds later. The max g-force felt by the crew will be 6.8 g's. A second g spike of about 4.2 will be noted about four, five minutes later. The total blackout we're predicting this morning is on the order of three minutes. But since we have very little experience reentering at these velocities, we must caution you that those are only estimates."

It was all so informal—the list of events that would happen in a predictable order, the g-forces that would be merely *noted* by the crew. But for Haney to say that NASA had "very little experience reentering at these velocities" was like saying that until *Apollo 8*, human beings had very little experience flying to the moon. In fact, they had had none.

Inside the ship, the astronauts kept their tone equally nonchalant. Lovell looked through his window and noticed the way the onion skin of the atmosphere now looked so much thicker—thick enough that the sun shining through it broke into a spectrum of shades from the black of space to deep blue, then red, orange and finally bright yellow. Just three Christmases before, he and Borman had spent fourteen days with that rainbow ribbon outside their window; Anders, who had been extremely busy during *Apollo 8*'s brief stay in Earth orbit six days ago, had likely not seen it at all.

"I got the old . . . ," Lovell began, waving his hand toward the window.

"What is that?" Anders asked.

"Good old airglow is what it is," Borman said.

Anders glanced at it; unimpressed, he looked back down at his flight plan. "I'll look at the airglow next time," he said.

Lovell pressed: "You've never seen the airglow. Take a look at it."

"You can't get your pin without seeing the airglow," Borman teased, echoing the flight attendants on airplanes who would bribe restless children into good behavior with the promise of a gift of souvenir pilot's wings.

"That's right," Lovell said.

"I see it, I see it!" Anders laughed, making a show of gaping out the window. Then he affected the nervous look of the rookie pilot. "Let's see, is this where I'm supposed to ask, 'How many g's, Lovell?'"

Anders could joke, but the fact was, the g needle on the instrument panel had indeed begun to twitch. Meanwhile, the airglow was growing bright enough to reflect off the windows. The reflection quickly grew brighter and redder, the first sign that the ship was encountering air resistance.

At that moment, NASA radioed up a reminder to the crew to turn on the radar transponder that the recovery ships would need to track the spacecraft as it fell. But Mission Control would have to trust that the astronauts had heard the command and obeyed it, because the instant the words were uttered, the communications link was cut.

"And we have lost signal," Haney announced.

* * * * * * * *

Lovell didn't need a mission commentator to tell him what the hiss in his headset already had. The crew was alone once more. He turned to Anders.

"You've got the checklist again, Bill?" he asked.

"You've got it?" Borman repeated.

"Yes," Anders assured them, holding up the flight plan.

"I'll tell you when the g's start going," Lovell said, the matter no longer a subject of humor.

"This is going to be a real ride; hang on," Borman said, then turned to Lovell. "You got point-zero-five g?" That reading— just five-hundredths of a single g—would be the first data reading indicating that reentry had officially begun.

"I've got point-zero-two," Lovell said.

A stray washer, missed in the cleanup but now with a tiny bit of weight to it, drifted into view, falling in slow motion.

"There goes a washer," Borman said. "Can you grab it?"

Before anyone could get it, the little bit of junk floated off again.

Lovell's eyes remained on his instruments, watching both his g-meter and the mission clock. He knew precisely how the joint forces of gravity and time were supposed to play out. And then: "Point-zero-five!"

"Point-zero-five," Borman confirmed.

"Okay, we got it!" Anders said.

"Hang on!" Borman called.

"They're building up," Lovell said.

"Call out the g's," Borman commanded.

"We're at one g!" Lovell called.

The astronauts stayed silent for just twenty seconds as the g-forces rapidly multiplied. Lovell watched the needle climb to two, then three, then four and beyond.

"Five," he said, straining to get out the syllable as a force quintuple Earth's nominal gravity pressed down on his chest. Then yet another rock was piled on.

"Six," he said through his teeth.

The red glow outside the spacecraft brightened to the orange of a roaring fire, then to deep yellow, then brilliant yellow, then a pure, near-blinding white. The astronauts squinted against it; the light was so intense that Borman felt as if he were inside a fluorescent bulb. As the white light, which had no other degree of brightness left to it, held steady, the g's, which knew no such limits, climbed to a peak of 6.84.

Then, at last, the roller coaster rose according to the plan and the g's started backing off.

"Four," Lovell said, relieved at that minimal easing of the pressure.

"Quite a ride, huh?" Anders said.

A moment later, Lovell, breathing more easily still, provided another report. "We're below two g's," he said.

"Nice job there, gang," Borman said.

The break would not last. The final dive was yet to come, when the g's would climb back over four. The astronauts were still more than thirty-three miles above the Earth and free-falling through the sky. Not until 24,000 feet would the two thirteen-foot-diameter parachutes be deployed, jerking the spacecraft to a slower, but still lethal, 200 miles per hour. Only at 10,000 feet would the three main chutes, each 83.5 feet across, open up, braking the spacecraft to a tolerable landing speed.

Even then, "tolerable" was a relative notion. The spacecraft would hit the water at just over twenty-one miles per hour, which seems like nothing when you've been flying a ship that just minutes before was moving at one thousand times that speed. But twenty-one miles per hour is a speed that on impact makes water feel like a solid and shakes you with a force that rattles your teeth.

But all that was for when *Apollo 8* was a lot closer to the Earth and moving a lot slower than it was right now.

✴ ✴ ✴ ✴ ✴ ✴ ✴ ✴

Far below the spacecraft, rescue helicopters had already begun scrambling from the deck of the USS *Yorktown* in the Pacific, converging on the site where the command module was likely to splash down. Once the rescue teams arrived, there would be nothing for them to do but hover and station-keep.

For now, *Apollo 8* still hadn't emerged from blackout. In the Borman, Lovell and Anders homes, the only sounds came from the television sets and the squawk boxes. The children—eleven of them among the three families—were all awake, and those who were old enough to understand what was happening were watching the coverage on TV. For these final moments of the mission all three mothers were sitting in their living rooms, their children close by.

The blackout stretched to four and a half minutes and then closed on five.

"It's now just two minutes past the time we should have heard from the spacecraft," Cronkite said somberly.

"Houston, *Apollo 8*, through Huntsville," Mattingly called.

He allowed almost another minute to pass.

"*Apollo 8, Apollo 8*, this Houston," he tried once more.

Fifteen more seconds of silence elapsed.

Then, at last, through the loud wash of air-to-ground static, Jim Lovell's voice—broken but discernible—filled the Mission Control headsets and the living rooms around the planet.

"Houston, *Apollo 8*, over," he said.

"And . . . ," Haney began, his voice choking before he took a second breath, "there's Jim Lovell!"

"Ha ha!" Cronkite exclaimed.

"Go ahead, *Apollo 8*, read you broken and loud," said Mattingly.

"Roger," Borman shouted back through the crackle and roar of the plasma cloud only now dissipating from around the ship. "This is a real fireball! It's looking good!"

"He says we're looking good!" Haney said.

Borman looked out his forward window. "There she comes!" he said, as the conical nose of the capsule blew away and the two red-and-white parachutes reefed and bloomed.

The astronauts jerked back in their couches, but the tenuous communications link had broken off again and the crew did not even bother to call the ground to confirm the chute deployment.

At just over the promised altitude of 10,000 feet, the main chutes burst free. The men jerked once more and the ship's descent slowed dramatically.

The communications loop opened up again and another voice—an entirely new one—filled their headsets.

"This is Air Boss 1," someone announced, using the call signal of a rescue helicopter. The unmistakable sound of rotor blades chopped in the background. "You're sounding very good, very good. You have been reported on radar as southwest of the ship, about twenty-five miles."

"Roger," Lovell answered.

The spacecraft fell through 8,000 and 6,000 and then just 5,000 feet. After a journey of half a million miles, the ship was now less than a mile above the water.

"The spacecraft is down to one thousand," the pilot of the helicopter called to the *Yorktown*.

"Brace yourselves," Borman called to Lovell and Anders.

"Welcome home, gentlemen," the pilot said, a few seconds prematurely. "We'll have you aboard in no time."

"Stand by," Borman said to his crew. "Stand by for Earth landing."

A moment later, the three astronauts felt the hard hand of the Earth's surface hit them at their backs as their spacecraft half sliced, half slammed into the rolling waters of the Pacific Ocean, the jolt violent.

The crew barely noticed. Borman pumped his fist, Lovell

and Anders let out a whoop and all three men looked at one another and grinned.

"*Yorktown*, Recovery 3," a helicopter pilot called. "At this time the spacecraft is in the water."

Walter Cronkite, his voice filled with relief and jubilation, made it official. "The spacecraft *Apollo 8* is back!"

* * * * * * * *

And so it was. But getting the spacecraft into the ocean was not the same as getting the astronauts onto the carrier.

It would not be difficult to find *Apollo 8* in the predawn darkness, thanks to both the flashing white light on the nose of the ship and the radar beacon that had been pinging throughout reentry. But Pacific sharks prowl during the early morning hours, and nobody wanted to take the chance that either the moon men or the frogmen would attract their deadly attention. So the astronauts would have to bob and drift in their airtight pod in six-foot waves for a while. Once the skies brightened, it would take another hour for the frogmen to hit the water and attach a flotation collar to the spacecraft, which would make it possible for the astronauts to leave their ship without falling into the sea. Only then could the hatch be opened and the crew extracted, at which point the men would be lifted one by one up to the helicopter that would fly them back to the *Yorktown*.

The wait for their rescuers would not be pleasant. The cabin temperature was now sweltering, both from the fiery descent through the atmosphere and the warm temperatures in the

South Pacific. The combination of the two—hot, close air and the heaving of the capsule—did not do good things to a pilot's insides.

Making the crew's circumstances worse, the motion of the waves soon caused the spacecraft to flip from the position that NASA called "stable one" to the position called "stable two"—what anyone else would call right-side up to upside down. That left the astronauts hanging in their straps in the now unfamiliar one-g environment, looking down at their instrument panel. Borman could activate three flotation balloons packed in the nose of the spacecraft near where the parachutes had been, and he promptly did so. But it would take a while for the balloons to turn the spacecraft back over. Both Mission Control and the recovery helicopters noticed relatively little chatter coming from the spacecraft, a silence characteristic of anyone battling a rising bubble of nausea.

"Get us out of here," Anders finally radioed, only partly joking. "I'm not the sailor on this boat."

Lovell, the navy man flying with two air force men, managed to keep any seasickness in check. So did Anders. Borman, who had begun his mission to the moon fighting a losing battle against his rebellious stomach, lost again. If the *Apollo 8* spacecraft was destined for a museum—which it surely was—the conservators would have a little cleanup work to do first.

Eventually, the sky did brighten, the choppers closed in and the frogmen leapt into the water. They waved at the crew through windows that less than seventy-two hours before had been filled with the bright, bleak landscape of the moon; now, seeing the faces of smiling strangers, the astronauts waved back. Once the flotation collar was secured, one of the frogmen signaled the all clear by banging on the hatch. Lovell, in the center position—the position occupied by Ed White in a different ship almost two long years ago—opened the little door with ease.

The fresh smell and warm breeze of the Pacific flowed into the capsule, replacing the stuffy air the crew had been breathing for nearly a week.

"Welcome home, men," the lead frogman said.

The astronauts were helped out of the spacecraft, onto the docking collar and into a life raft. As a helicopter hovered noisily overhead, a rescue basket lifted them to safety. The chopper's crew saluted each man as he climbed aboard.

"Congratulations, sir," said Donald Jones, the pilot, to Borman. "It was a wonderful reentry."

Borman demurred. "It was all automatic," he said. "We had nothing to do with it."

The commander of the first mission to the moon was pretty sure he would be congratulated and applauded a lot in the coming weeks, but he had already decided that he would take credit for only the accomplishments that were actually his.

When the helicopter at last landed on the *Yorktown*'s deck, a red carpet was waiting. The door opened and the astronauts emerged, grinning and waving as the carrier's crew cheered. In Houston, the Mission Controllers had scrupulously abided by the rule that no celebration would be permitted until that moment. When they saw the astronauts appear, they too shouted and hugged and shook hands.

The astronauts walked between the ranks of cheering sailors, waving and calling out thank-yous. At the end of the carpet, they were greeted by Captain John Field, the commander of the ship, who presented them with USS *Yorktown* baseball caps, which they donned as demanded by both tradition and a genuine gratitude for the efforts that had been made on their behalf. The astronauts shook hands with Field, who then motioned Borman to a standing microphone that had been placed there for him.

Though Borman had not prepared a speech, he welcomed the chance to show his appreciation to the carrier's crew.

"It seems that Jim and I always fly in December, doesn't it?" he said to appreciative laughter from the ship's crew. "That time we got back before Christmas. This time we didn't and we want to apologize for keeping you out here over the holidays."

After a few more remarks and thank-yous, the astronauts vanished belowdecks to the sick bay for their post-flight medical exams. There would be a call to take from President Johnson and another from Vice President Humphrey, and already congratulatory statements and telegrams were streaming in to the astronauts from world leaders. Russian leaders sent congratulations; in fact the White House had used the Washington-Moscow hotline—installed mostly as a direct source of communication during times of military escalation—to keep the Soviets apprised of the status of the mission.

"Accept, Mr. President, our congratulations on the successful completion of the flight of the *Apollo 8* spacecraft around the moon," said Soviet President Nikolai Podgorny in his formal statement to Lyndon Johnson. The mission, Podgorny said, "is a new accomplishment in mastering the outer space by man." The telegram implicitly acknowledged that the United States had just won a dramatic battle in the Cold War, and the official spokesman for the opponent was—grudgingly perhaps, but graciously—conceding that fact. In a contest so often marked by ambiguous outcomes, *Apollo 8* had scored a clear victory.

Belowdecks, freshly showered, the astronauts had changed into clean white flight suits, combed their hair, and donned their *Yorktown* caps. They then climbed the metal ladder back to the deck. By now, their spacecraft had been hauled aboard and the portion of the deck that held the little capsule had been cordoned off.

The astronauts approached their spacecraft and examined it. By any measure, the ship was spent. Its sides were discolored by the fires of the reentry, and its heat shield was half incinerated. Its tapered nose had been jettisoned to allow the parachutes and flotation balloons to deploy, giving the front of the capsule an incomplete, even broken look.

The hatch was partly open and the men looked inside. It was a cluttered mess. There would be a few souvenirs to collect—the flight plans, a flashlight. But the command module was now retired, an artifact of history.

Jim Lovell and Bill Anders regarded their spacecraft with an acute feeling of unfinished business. If given the chance, they would take another ship—tomorrow wouldn't be too soon—and fly the whole mission again, only this time they would land on the moon they had so recently orbited.

Frank Borman felt nothing of the kind. He had been assigned a mission, he had flown the mission and he had come home from the mission. He gave the scarred side of the command module an affectionate slap, then turned around and walked away. He did not look back.

• EPILOGUE •

THE COUNTRY'S CELEBRATION of the astronauts' achievement had begun almost the moment they returned to Earth, and it would continue for a good while. The astronauts met President Johnson in the White House and were awarded NASA's Distinguished Service Medal. They were also invited to address the United States Congress, where Borman thanked the legislators for funding the space program and urged them to continue supporting it, saying, "Exploration is really the essence of the human spirit, and I hope we will never forget that."

The astronauts were driven down Pennsylvania Avenue in Washington, DC, in a motorcade while a great crowd of people waved and cheered. The astronauts' families, who were invited to attend all the events, rode in trailing cars behind the motorcade.

Marveling at the throngs of people, seven-year-old Susan Lovell turned to her mother. "You'd think Dad was a hero or something," she said.

"Well, Susan," Marilyn answered, "I think he is."

All three of the heroes got much the same treatment in New York the next day. There was a ticker-tape parade, with all of the street signs along the route changed temporarily to Apollo Way. As their procession crept along lower Broadway in a twenty-eight-degree chill, two hundred tons of confetti fluttered down on the astronauts.

In Houston, the technicians and Mission Controllers partied at a local restaurant. Leaving their cars parked up and down the four-lane stretch of highway, they swarmed inside. Those who couldn't find even one of those barely legal parking spaces simply abandoned their cars on the median strip; the Houston police, for whom it was still just another regular night, ticketed them with abandon.

But at NASA itself, the work continued, and for some, it started just hours after Borman, Lovell and Anders splashed down when a team of flight directors began simulations for *Apollo 9*.

On March 3, 1969—just over nine weeks later—astronauts flew *Apollo 9*, which included a successful test of the untried lunar module. At long last, the spindly ship that had given engineers such fits was declared fit for service.

Apollo 10 followed two months later, and then, two months after that, the American space program landed two men on the moon. *Apollo 11* was, as Neil Armstrong intoned, ". . . one small step for a man, one giant leap for mankind." Taking seriously their duty as emissaries to the moon for our species, Armstrong and Buzz Aldrin left behind a few tokens of Earthly goodwill and international fellowship: medallions commemorating astronauts who had perished in the line of duty—two Soviet cosmonauts and the three Americans who died in the *Apollo* blast two years prior—and a disk bearing messages of peace from seventy-three countries for whatever extraterrestrial beings might stumble upon it someday.

✷ ✷ ✷ ✷ ✷ ✷ ✷ ✷

Space and lunar exploration continued apace. The Apollo program launched another six lunar missions, and NASA invented new ways to leave our mark on the heavens. In 1981, it inaugurated its space shuttle program, which showcased a flying machine that could lift off with the help of rockets and land back on Earth like a glider. This unique design made the shuttle reusable, and its five orbiters were in heavy rotation for the next thirty years, logging over half a billion miles during 135 missions. The shuttle launched the first American woman into space as well as the first African American. In all, the shuttle program sent 350 men and women into space, where they repaired satellites and built the International Space Station (ISS), a football field-size lab that orbits the Earth every ninety minutes. Crews from around the world conduct experiments on the ISS, and if you look up into the sky on a clear night, even without using a telescope, you can see it fly by.

But over the years, the space program experienced tragic losses, too. In January 1986, the world excitedly watched as the space shuttle *Challenger* got ready to launch a crew that included Christa McAuliffe, a social-studies teacher. Astronauts were considered almost superhuman: physically fit math and science whizzes who were perfectly trained, cool under pressure and could defy gravity and fly at dizzying speeds. But Christa

McAuliffe was one of us. This was the first time a regular teacher had been selected to join the crew, and she had spent months training for what was dubbed "the ultimate field trip."

Bundled up in the stands on that cold January day were Christa McAuliffe's parents and her sister; her husband and children were watching from inside a building nearby. They were joined by one in six Americans who tuned into the launch on TV, including millions of schoolchildren, cheering for one of their own.

And then, just seventy-three seconds after liftoff, the *Challenger* exploded in midair, killing its seven-member crew and halting shuttle flights for two years. While other shuttles had many successes, in 2003 tragedy again struck when the *Columbia* space shuttle broke apart as it was reentering the Earth's atmosphere after orbiting the planet for two weeks. Once again, NASA lost seven crew members.

For all of NASA's spectacular triumphs, the public and press tended to focus on its disasters, when they paid attention at all. Maybe people grew skittish about the risks of spaceflight. Maybe they were worried that NASA was wasting scarce government funds. Once America officially beat the Soviet Union in the Cold War in 1989, the urgency of the space race melted away. America was now the world's one and only superpower, so why did we still need to pour billions into the space program? Don't we have bigger problems to solve here at home, where our money could be better spent?

In the short term, the answer will always be yes. In our country and around the world, there are millions of hungry mouths to feed and homeless people in need of shelter. There are deadly diseases to cure urgently and unemployed workers who need immediate assistance. There are roads to be paved and bridges to be fixed today.

But what if all the resources we pour into rocket design and flight planning also make life on Earth better, more interesting, safer and healthier? The most famous by-product of the Cold War is none other than our beloved, unwieldy, babbling Internet, the platform that changed human engagement forever. No longer is communication just one-to-one, as it is through the telephone, or even the broadcast of a few to the many, as through TV and radio. The Internet has made it possible for all to speak to all and all at once, a revolution in the dynamics of power and community we are still trying to master as we ride this beast in our every waking moment.

Advances discovered in NASA labs have become a part of our daily lives, too. Rocket technology powers heart pumps, and infant formula is fortified with nutrients that NASA developed for long-duration spaceflight. Your sunglasses, baseball bat, tennis racquet and even the mattress you sleep on at night have been improved by the space agency.

But what if we got nothing at all from the research at NASA? No special sunlight filters for your shades, no added cushioning for your memory-foam pillow. Would all of it be worth it? The trips to the moon, the billions of dollars and countless human-hours spent contemplating, exploring the vast, endless night? The lives lost?

In 1961, President Kennedy nudged Americans "with the

full speed of freedom" to shoulder the burden of a massive project. President Kennedy asked Americans to be bold and choose to go to the moon. In a speech before Congress, he clearly laid out the costs in dollars and time and resources and manpower and asked citizens to think hard about their willingness to take on the moon shot, acknowledging that "no one can predict with certainty what the ultimate meaning will be of mastery of space." Certainly no one could predict that just two years after his call, he would be assassinated, and five years after that the country would bleed and burn in the fires of 1967 and 1968.

But he could predict that if Americans sent a man to the moon, we would all be able to bask in its glow for generations to come, that such a show of resolve and dedication, shared purpose and courage would offer a road map for future Americans who might again be faced with questions about how much we should all expect to contribute to a great leap for humanity, how seriously we take our responsibility to lead. "In a very real sense," Kennedy said, "it will not be one man going to the moon—if we make this judgment affirmatively, it will be an entire nation. For all of us must work to put him there."

APOLLO 8 GLOSSARY

AGENA: early uncrewed spacecraft

APOLLO: three-person spacecraft designed to fly to the moon

ATTITUDE: the way the ship is pointed

BOOSTER: another word for a rocket

BURN: When a rocket's engines light, it is called a burn, because it is burning fuel.

CAPCOM: The person in Mission Control who radios up all information to the crew. The capcom is always an astronaut who is not flying on the current mission; the name is short for capsule communicator.

CAPE KENNEDY: The launch site for spacecraft. Originally called Cape Canaveral.

CIRCUMLUNAR: A flight that whips around the back of the moon and comes home without orbiting. It is the moon's gravity that tosses the spacecraft back to Earth.

COMMAND-SERVICE MODULE (CSM): The cone-shaped portion of the spacecraft that houses the crew is the command module; the astronauts and all the controls on their instrument panel command where the spaceship goes and what it does. The service portion is a cylindrical, twenty-four-foot structure attached to the rear of the command module like the trailer behind the cab of a truck. It contains the spacecraft's main engine, the SPS, as well as much of its essential hardware, like oxygen tanks, water supply and batteries and fuel cells.

ENGINE BELL: The bell-shaped structure that protrudes from the back of the service module and helps direct the engine's fire. There are engine bells at the bottom of rockets, too.

FLIGHT DIRECTOR: the boss of Mission Control, responsible for all final decisions throughout a flight

FLIGHT DYNAMICS (FIDO): the Mission Control console operator who managed the trajectory, or route, of the rocket and the *Apollo* spacecraft

FLIGHT PLAN: a detailed plan of every moment of the mission and the roles of every player on the ground and in the air

GANTRY: a tall, moveable, towerlike structure with a platform that supports the rocket and *Apollo* when they're on the launchpad

GEMINI: two-person spacecraft designed for Earth orbit

JETTISON: let go or get rid of

LOSS OF SIGNAL (LOS): When an object blocks radio waves between a spacecraft and Earth, communication is lost.

LUNAR EXCURSION MODULE (LEM): A two-part ship. Its first task would be to land on the moon with its four legs and a powerful descent engine. When it was time to take off, the bottom half of the ship would serve as a launch platform, with explosive bolts and a guillotine system cutting the cables and other links to the top half, allowing an ascent engine to carry the remains of the spacecraft—which was essentially the crew cabin—up to lunar orbit.

LUNAR ORBIT INSERTION (LOI): the burn the *Apollo*'s main engine—known as the SPS—makes to settle the *Apollo* into orbit around the moon

MANNED: A mission that has humans aboard operating the craft. Today we say "crewed" since both men and women fly in space.

MERCURY: America's first crewed spacecraft, designed for one person

MISSION CONTROL: The large auditorium-like room at the NASA space center in Houston where the spaceflight is managed. It houses consoles with experts who track and manage every technical aspect of the flight.

MASCON: Short for "mass concentrations"—the remains of heavy-metal meteorites that long ago crashed into the moon and buried themselves there. They make lunar gravity uneven.

PASSIVE THERMAL CONTROL (PTC): A slow, one revolution-per-minute rotisserie roll that would be initiated with a single burn of the *Apollo* thrusters and would continue indefinitely until there was a counterthrust—or a burn in the other direction—when the craft is in zero-g. It kept the spacecraft evenly warmed by the sun on all sides

PITCH: When the nose of spacecraft moves up or down; a 360-degree pitch would thus be a somersault.

RETROFIRE: When a spacecraft turns backward and fires its engine in front of it as it flies. It is used to slow the spacecraft down.

ROCKET: a projectile that can shoot a spacecraft into space by igniting its combustible fuel

ROLL: Roll is when the spacecraft moves the way a can or other cylinder would if you lay it on its side and give it a push so it rolls along the floor.

SATURN V: massive, thirty-six-story, three-stage rocket that would blast the *Apollo* spacecraft moonward

SERVICE PROPULSION SYSTEM (SPS): Engine on *Apollo* spacecraft. Needed to work properly at least twice on an Apollo mission; once to get into lunar orbit, once to get out.

SIMSUP: Simulation supervisors. Their job is to introduce uncertainty and problems into simulations of flights so that the technicians and the astronauts will be ready for any problems that might arise.

STATION-KEEP: When two vehicles stay at a fixed distance from each other, moving neither closer nor farther apart.

SUSTAINER ENGINE CUTOFF (SECO): shutdown of the *Saturn V*'s third-stage engine, after it was lit to push the astronauts out of Earth orbit and send them to the moon

TELEMETRY: the computer data that always streams down from the spacecraft to Earth, telling the controllers how the mission is functioning

THRUSTERS: Little engines positioned on the outside of a spacecraft. They help it maneuver in different directions.

TITAN BOOSTER: rocket that launched *Gemini* spacecraft

TRANS-EARTH INJECTION (TEI): the burn of the rocket's engine that pushes a spacecraft out of lunar orbit and sends it back toward Earth

TRANSLUNAR INJECTION (TLI): the burn of a rocket that sends astronauts out of Earth orbit and out to the moon

VELOCITY: speed

YAW: Yaw is when the nose of a spacecraft waggles left or right; a 360-degree yaw would thus be a flat spin, moving around the way clock hands circle a clock face.

ZERO-G: In space, astronauts feel no gravitational pull, which allows them to float. One g is the gravitational environment of the Earth.

Apollo 8 *lifted off on time at 7:51 a.m. EST on December 21, 1968. The* Saturn V *rocket stood 363 feet tall—about the same as a thirty-six-story building.*

The night before launch, the Apollo 8 *moon rocket was brilliantly illuminated by floodlights. It was visible from nearly three miles away.*

The Apollo *spacecraft—seen here in the factory—was a two-part ship: the cone-shaped command module, which housed the crew, was in front; the cylindrical service module, which contained fuel tanks and life support systems, was behind. The engine bell protruded from the back.*

The first stage of the Saturn V was 138 feet tall and contained the rocket's five most powerful engines. Here it is seen in its Louisiana assembly facility.

In the 1960s, NASA released an illustration showing how remarkable the Saturn V was. The cutaway diagram reveals the fuel tanks and other components. The space agency reminded people that the Saturn V was taller than the Statue of Liberty and produced more energy than eighty-five Hoover Dams.

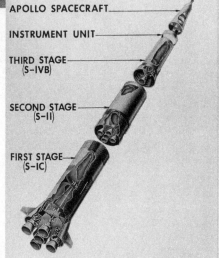

APOLLO SPACECRAFT

INSTRUMENT UNIT

THIRD STAGE (S–IVB)

SECOND STAGE (S–II)

FIRST STAGE (S–IC)

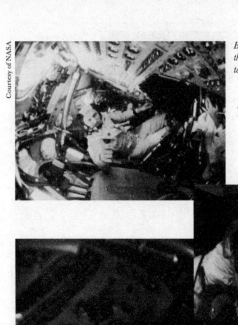

Borman, captured in a frame from the sixteen-millimeter onboard movie taken by the Apollo 8 crew.

Lovell, sighting stars at his navigation station, in a frame from the sixteen-millimeter movie.

Anders, in a frame from the same footage, showing a generous growth of beard, which suggests that the image was captured more than halfway through the mission.

ΛPOLLO COMMΛND MODULE INTERIOR

LEFT SIDE

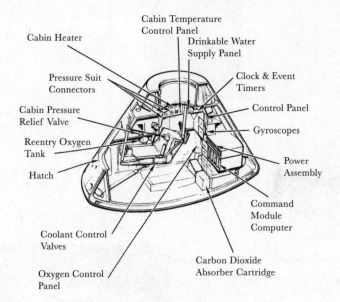

Cabin Heater

Cabin Temperature
Control Panel

Drinkable Water
Supply Panel

Pressure Suit
Connectors

Clock & Event
Timers

Cabin Pressure
Relief Valve

Control Panel

Reentry Oxygen
Tank

Gyroscopes

Hatch

Power
Assembly

Command
Module
Computer

Coolant Control
Valves

Carbon Dioxide
Absorber Cartridge

Oxygen Control
Panel

RIGHT SIDE

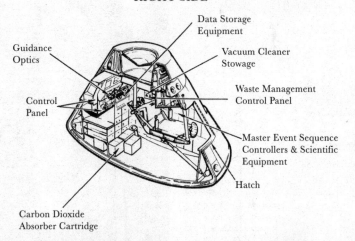

Data Storage
Equipment

Guidance
Optics

Vacuum Cleaner
Stowage

Waste Management
Control Panel

Control
Panel

Master Event Sequence
Controllers & Scientific
Equipment

Hatch

Carbon Dioxide
Absorber Cartridge

Courtesy of NASA

The eleven-foot-tall command module was all that remained of the 363-foot Saturn V rocket at the end of the mission.
It was home to the Apollo 8 astronauts for their entire journey—a little like being inside a minivan for six days.

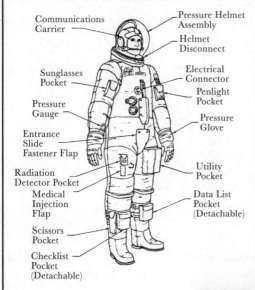

Communications Carrier

Pressure Helmet Assembly

Helmet Disconnect

Sunglasses Pocket

Electrical Connector

Penlight Pocket

Pressure Gauge

Pressure Glove

Entrance Slide Fastener Flap

Radiation Detector Pocket

Utility Pocket

Medical Injection Flap

Data List Pocket (Detachable)

Scissors Pocket

Checklist Pocket (Detachable)

NASA's diagrams showed how complicated the astronauts' space suits were, with many layers and utility pockets as well as ports so that oxygen and air-conditioning hoses could be attached.

The space suit Bill Anders wore during the Apollo 8 mission traveled all the way to the moon and back, and now lives forever in Washington, DC, part of the Smithsonian Museum's space collection.

Lovell, Anders and Borman (left to right) posed in front of the Apollo simulator where they spent a great deal of their time during training. Inside, the simulator is a working mock-up of their Apollo command module, allowing the crew to practice procedures and learn how to handle emergencies.

Following their splashdown, the Apollo 8 *crew (left to right, Borman, Lovell and Anders) climbed out of their spacecraft and a helicopter carried them safely to the* USS *Yorktown, where they emerged and waved to the crew. The spacecraft was brought aboard the ship later.*

Like much of the rest of the world, the team in Mission Control in Houston watched the astronauts' broadcast on the third day of their journey. The Earth—which no one had ever seen from such a distance before—is visible on the screen at the front of the room.

(left) Gene Kranz was the highest-ranking flight director in Mission Control. He helped lead NASA's recovery from the Apollo 1 fire and was one of the key people involved in planning Apollo 8. Here he is seen during a Gemini IV simulation in 1965.

(right) Chris Kraft was the director of flight operations and one of the first people who had to approve of the Apollo 8 mission before it could be flown at all. Here he is seen three years earlier in Mission Control, working as flight director during the Gemini IV flight in 1965.

Chief astronaut Deke Slayton (center) compares images of the moon sent back by a robot probe to the ones the Apollo 8 was sending back from lunar orbit. He is surrounded (clockwise) by astronauts Gerald Carr, Harrison Schmitt, Buzz Aldrin and Neil Armstrong. Seven months later, Armstrong would become the first man on the moon and Aldrin the second.

On the third of their ten orbits, the Apollo 8 astronauts got their first glimpse of the Earth rising over the moon. They had to move fast to capture the image before the Earth drifted out of frame. The historic shot became known simply as "Earthrise," and would be credited with helping to launch the environmental movement.

The Apollo 8 patch, devised by Lovell, was perhaps the cleverest of all of the Apollo missions' insignias. The numeral "8" roughly tracks the flight path the astronauts flew around the Earth and the moon, though it doesn't show that they completely orbited both worlds.

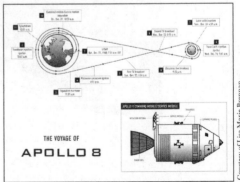

THE VOYAGE OF

APOLLO 8

The Lovell family: Jim (far right), his wife, Marilyn (far left), and their children (clockwise from top), Jay, Barbara, Jeffrey and Susan.

(above) The Borman family, photographed in the months before Apollo 8's launch: Frank (right), his wife, Susan (seated), and their sons, Fred (left) and Ed.

(right) The Anders family: Bill (top left), his wife, Valerie (center), and their children (clockwise from top), Gregory, Alan, Glen, Gayle and Eric.

The Original Seven astronauts, in 1960. Back row: Al Shepard, Gus Grissom, Gordon Cooper; front row: Wally Schirra, Deke Slayton, John Glenn, Scott Carpenter. Not all of the space suits were ready on the day the picture was taken, so Slayton and Glenn are wearing spray-painted work boots.

The second class of astronauts, chosen by NASA in 1962. Kneeling left to right are, Pete Conrad, Frank Borman, Neil Armstrong and John Young; Behind them are Elliot See, Jim McDivitt, Jim Lovell, Ed White and Tom Stafford.

Although it was past 2:00 a.m. on Dec. 29, 1968, more than 2,000 people were on hand at Ellington Air Force Base in Houston to welcome the members of the Apollo 8 crew home. The three astronauts are standing at the microphones in center of the picture.

50 YEARS LATER: REFLECTING BACK WITH THE *APOLLO 8* ASTRONAUTS

There's no record of the first time Frank Borman, Jim Lovell and Bill Anders first saw their *Apollo 8* spacecraft. It's a certainty they didn't call it *Apollo 8* back then. What they called it was Apollo CSM-103. The CSM stood for command-service module—the two parts of the spacecraft that they eventually flew to the moon. And the 103 was simply the code number by which the spacecraft was known when it was built in the North American Aviation factory in Downey, California.

It was only later, when the crews were assigned to a particular spacecraft and the spacecraft was assigned a specific mission, that a ship would get its name. In the case of the ship Borman, Lovell and Anders got, that name was *Apollo 8,* and the mission was the first human flight to the moon.

If there is no way of knowing exactly what unfolded the day they met their celebrated ship, there is an extensive record of the most recent time all three astronauts visited it. That happened on October 6, 2018, when the crew traveled to the Museum of Science and Industry in Chicago, where the spacecraft is on display and where Borman, Lovell and Anders were being honored in a gala event as the 50th anniversary of the mission approached.

Machines tend to age better than human beings do, and the spacecraft looks little different from the way it did on December 27, 1968, when it was hauled from the Pacific Ocean after its splashdown, and gently deposited on the deck of the aircraft carrier USS *Yorktown*. The astronauts themselves—Borman and Lovell, both 90, and Anders, 84—do show the years. The three great fliers move more slowly than they did when they set out to explore the moon so long ago.

"We had a heck of a time climbing into that car," Borman jokes as he gets out of the limousine that brought the three men to the museum. For a man who spent a lifetime climbing into and out of spacecraft and aircraft, the limo was just one more machine that had to be mastered, and if it's harder these days than it used to be, well, what of it?

Still, some things about veteran pilots who flew together and faced danger together never changes. They don't tire of needling one another, for one thing. It was Anders, the rookie of the crew back then, who took the now-famous picture known as *Earthrise*—the first glimpse of the blue-white Earth coming up over the ash-gray moon. History recognizes Anders's authorship of the picture and the audio transcripts of the mission confirm it. But the two senior astronauts will never quite give the junior crewman peace.

"I'm still trying to figure out who took that picture," Borman says when the topic comes up.

"Frank took it, I think," Lovell answers.

"Bill took the picture with a 250-millimeter lens, right?" Borman concedes, giving his one-time junior crewman the credit he deserves.

But Anders almost didn't take the picture at all, since it was up to the commander to schedule the photography times, and the Earth appeared over the horizon when pictures weren't planned.

"He didn't want me to take it!" jokes Anders, about Borman.

They joke as well when they talk about NASA, which managed to get to the moon so quickly and triumphantly in the 1960s, but hasn't been back there since 1972—and certainly is nowhere near achieving its professed dream of one day going to Mars. Anders is blunt in describing his frustration with that and then catches himself.

"We sound like we're old, but we are," he says.

"You're grumpy," Borman says. "I'm not grumpy."

But their love of their mission is apparent—of the chance they took and the history they made when the three of them, alone among the 3.5 billion people on Earth at the time and first among all of the billions who ever lived on Earth through-out its entire history, glimpsed the far side of the moon, settled into orbit around it and became, for 20 hours, beings of another world. Lovell, it always seemed, flew for the pure joy of flight; Anders for the close-up study of the moon, helping to scout possible landing sites for crews that would come later. Borman flew unabashedly for his country, to beat the Soviet Union in the deadly rivalry that was known as the Cold War.

"The tensions were pretty high on *Apollo 8*," he says. "It was a battle in the Cold War and the fact is, the Apollo program was a uniquely American program." Still, Borman observes that once that battle was won, once Americans became the first to reach the moon, the next step—actually walking on the moon, which came with *Apollo 11* seven months later—was more of a global achievement. "When we came to the moon in *Apollo 11*, finally," he says, "we came for all mankind."

That, of course, was the true legacy of *Apollo 8* too—the humanness of it, the unexpected earthliness of it. Borman spoke to me once, a few years ago, about his first close-up view of the moon, and how the old, barren world left him strangely unmoved.

"I had no particular emotions looking at the moon," he said. "It was just part of the deal. I had emotions looking at the Earth."

That feeling, that sense of being touched less by the world he was visiting than the one he had left, stays with him now, fifty years after he came home. And it's a feeling that carries a powerful insight for the now 7.5 billion people on the planet.

"I looked at the Earth from the moon and it was about the size of a fist held at arm's length," he says, "and I'm thinking, 'This is not a very big place, you know. Why can't we all get along?'"

In the years since the Cold War, there have been—and continue to be—many hot wars. The combatants have changed, the nations themselves have changed, but Borman's simple lesson from the mission he commanded will forever remain the same.

The Apollo 8 crew—left to right: Anders, Borman and Lovell—gathered in front of their old spacecraft in Chicago's Museum of Science and Industry on October 6, 2018. The hatch remains open to give museum-goers a look inside the ship in which the men made history.

AUTHOR'S NOTE

Though *To the Moon!* is written in a novelistic style, it is entirely nonfiction, and all of the conversations among the characters are authentic. Exchanges between the spacecraft and the ground or between the astronauts themselves during flight were drawn from NASA transcripts and recordings, which are readily available online through the Johnson Space Center History Office. In some cases, the exchanges were edited or compressed for clarity and readability; in no event was the meaning or context changed. All conversations for which there is no recording or transcript were reconstructed through interviews I conducted with the people involved, through their autobiographies, or with the help of NASA oral history interviews, which are also available on the NASA website. Confidential exchanges in the Soviet Union's Central Scientific Research Institute Building were originally reported in Volume 4 of Boris Chertok's four-volume set, *Rockets and People*. Some conversations and quotes were also drawn from newspapers, magazines, original reporting from the archives of *Time* magazine, and from the files at the Lyndon Baines Johnson Library and Museum in Austin, Texas.

In *Apollo 8*, the adult version of *To the Moon!*, I relied on the same research techniques. Jim Lovell and I used those methods as well in our collaboration, *Apollo 13*, and I did the same in my 2005 book, *Splendid Solution: Jonas Salk and the Conquest of Polio*. All history is, at bottom, a human tale, and is often most effectively told as the gripping nonfiction narrative it is.

INDEX

READ ON FOR A SAMPLE OF
JEFFREY KLUGER'S
THRILLING COLLECTION OF
SPACE MISSIONS GONE WRONG,

DISASTER STRIKES!

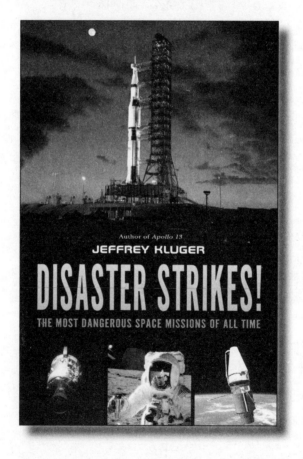

› TWO ›

SPINOUT IN SPACE

Gemini 8, 1966

NEIL ARMSTRONG DIDN'T believe in omens, but he got a nasty one anyway the moment he climbed into his *Gemini 8* spacecraft on the morning of March 16, 1966. As it turned out, if Armstrong had believed in omens, he might have been better prepared for what the rest of the day held for him.

Armstrong had been in a *Gemini* spacecraft plenty of times before; he'd been an astronaut for four years now and had done an awful lot of training in the new, two-person spacecraft. By any measure it was a hot rod of a ship—so much bigger than the little one-person pod that was the *Mercury* spacecraft, and so much more maneuverable, too. You could ride in a *Mercury*— but you could fly a *Gemini*.

Today, Armstrong, the commander of the Gemini 8 mission, was scheduled to do a lot of flying. Halfway across Cape Canaveral, an *Atlas* rocket was standing and steaming on launchpad fourteen, ready to take off for orbit carrying an unmanned spacecraft called an *Agena*.

The *Agena* was a beast: a twenty-six-foot-long, three-and-a-half-ton satellite, carrying four more tons of explosive fuel. It had a rocket engine at one end and a docking port at the other.

At 10:00 a.m., the *Atlas* would blast off and carry the *Agena* to orbit. Just 100 minutes later, Armstrong, a rookie, and his copilot, Dave Scott, another first-timer, would take off and give chase. Finding the *Agena* in orbit, they would move in close and then dock the nose of their ship in the port of the target.

A maneuver like that had never been accomplished before—and that was a problem. Getting astronauts back from the moon would require just this kind of piloting finesse, since a lunar module leaving the lunar surface would have to find the *Apollo* mother ship waiting in orbit and successfully link up with it. If it couldn't, the astronauts would never make it home.

On launchpad nineteen, as Armstrong and Scott eased into the seats of their *Gemini* ship, which itself sat atop their eleven-story *Titan* rocket, fellow astronaut Pete Conrad helped them get settled in. His job at the moment was to fasten the clasps on the escape parachutes the crew would use if an emergency during launch required them to eject.

One of Armstrong's clasps, however, wouldn't close. Conrad peered at it and frowned.

"It's glue, Neil," he said.

Armstrong responded incredulously: "Glue?" he asked.

"Glue," Conrad repeated. Somehow, a technician or other member of the ground crew had dripped a glob of glue inside the workings of the latch. If it couldn't be cleared, *Gemini 8* couldn't fly. If *Gemini 8* couldn't fly, neither could the *Agena*. Two launches would be scrubbed because of a tenth of a teaspoon of goo that had somehow found its way into the wrong spot.

Conrad, trained in every single bit of the *Gemini* system, used the most low-tech tool he had at his disposal—his finger— to try to gouge out the mess. After multiple tries, he did it. Armstrong tested the clasp several times, flashed a thumbs-up and the flight was a go.

The relief in Mission Control was palpable, partly because this mission had a lot more riding on it than just its planned dance with the *Agena*, and the shoulder patch the astronauts designed as the emblem for their flight captured that—provided you could make any sense out of it. The patches for all of the other *Gemini* flights had featured some variation on the space- craft and the mission number and the names of the astronauts. Armstrong and Scott chose, instead, a pair of stars projecting a beam of light that burst into a rainbow of colors.

The star part made sense—maybe. There were two of them, so they must have represented the astronauts. But the rainbow? That, NASA explained when reporters asked—and plenty of them did—stood for the fact that this was a full-spectrum mission. There would be the rendezvous and docking, yes, but there would also be a suite of ten scientific experiments to con- duct, plus two space walks by Scott. In fact, one of the space walks would be so long—a full ninety minutes—that it would last for an entire orbit.

The newspapers had fun with that one, running headlines that read: DAVE SCOTT WILL BE THE FIRST MAN TO WALK AROUND THE WORLD!

The mission would last only three days, but a lot would be packed into that short time, and it all started off perfectly when the *Atlas-Agena* left launchpad fourteen precisely on time at 10:00 a.m. and raced to a near-circular orbit 146 miles up.

The *Gemini* spacecraft—with its little glue problem sorted out—followed 101 minutes later, and Armstrong and Scott were clearly enjoying the ride.

"Hey, how about that view!" Scott enthused as the rocket climbed.

"That's fantastic!" Armstrong answered, and then added, "Boy! Here we go!"

And there they went indeed. Less than ten minutes after leaving the launchpad in Florida, the astronauts were in orbit.

What followed would be six hours of some of the most pains-taking work the two crewmen had ever done, with Armstrong tweaking various combinations of the sixteen little thrusters arrayed around the ship, until slowly, over four complete orbits, they closed in on the *Agena*—though they still couldn't see it.

Finally, when the two spacecraft were just seventy-six miles apart, the astronauts saw something reflecting back at them.

Scott warned that it might just be a planet.

Mission Control said that it could be the star Sirius.

But it wasn't a planet and it wasn't Sirius, and as Armstrong and Scott grew closer and closer, the target grew bigger and brighter and revealed itself unmistakably as the

Agena spacecraft—a beautiful machine, precisely launched and waiting exactly where it was supposed to be.

Armstrong, at the controls of his *Gemini*, was having the time of his life.

"Man, it flies easy. I'd love to let you try it!" he said to Scott.

"I'll get my chance. It's up to you; you stick with it," Scott encouraged.

The *Gemini* edged closer and closer to the *Agena*, as Armstrong released mere breaths of propellant from his thrusters. Both spacecraft were moving at matching speeds of 17,500 miles per hour, but the *Gemini* could speed up or slow down by a few inches per second, which is all it takes in the business of docking in space.

"Okay, we're sitting at two feet out," Armstrong called as he began to close the final distance.

He then crept forward until he was just a foot away, and then just a few inches, and then the front of the *Gemini* settled into the port of the *Agena* and the docking latches snapped shut.

"Flight, we are docked!" Armstrong called.

In Mission Control, where the loudest sound was usually that of men murmuring into headsets, a chorus of whoops and cheers rang out as they hadn't since the very first American space flights.

NASA was one very big step closer to the moon.

Still, there were reasons to be wary—and the people at NASA knew it. The *Agena* might be a beautiful machine, but it was also known to be a temperamental one, given to occasional bouts of misbehavior, and that included problems with its engine and thrusters. While a certain degree of imperfection was acceptable in a spacecraft that wasn't carrying astronauts, it could be deadly when that spacecraft was linked up with another ship that was carrying them.

What's more, Mission Control wouldn't always know if something had gone awry in the ships. American spacecraft orbiting Earth were not in constant touch with the ground in Florida; rather, they relied on a necklace of tracking stations around the world—in California, Mexico, Bermuda, Australia, Hawaii and elsewhere. Between those radio footprints, there were long minutes of blackout.

At the Tenerife station in the Canary Islands, astronaut Jim Lovell, who was manning the communications console, knew as well as anyone else the risks Armstrong and Scott faced as they flew through their orbits still linked to the target vehicle. So he radioed up a warning.

"If you run into trouble and the attitude control system of the *Agena* goes wild, just turn it off and take control with the spacecraft," he said. The attitude referred to the direction the spacecraft was pointing. If that control system went wild, it meant the ship could tumble around, completely out of control.

Armstrong promised he would do just that. Then he and Scott slipped into blackout.

There was little for the crew to do in the fifteen minutes before reacquisition of signal. There would be no maneuvering while they were out of contact with the ground, so the time would be spent simply keeping the spacecraft at a stable attitude and perhaps resuming a meal they had begun in the six hours they had been chasing the other ship.

As Scott tried to finish perfectly terrible chicken and gravy served in a plastic pouch, and a dessert of brownies, he gazed out his window. It was entirely dark outside, since the astronauts were on the nighttime side of the planet, so there was no horizon below them to see. That made it hard to determine if their ship was remaining stable.

Scott glanced at the instrument panel at what was known as the eight ball—the attitude indicator that spun in all axes in response to any movement of the ship.

It was supposed to be stationary. It wasn't.

"Neil, we're in a bank," he said.

Armstrong glanced at the eight ball. Scott was right, only it was worse than a bank. The *Gemini-Agena* combination was drifting in two axes—both roll and yaw, which meant a spin around its nose-to-tail axis, as well as a rotation in its left-right orientation. The only thing missing was a pitch—or a head-over-heels tumble.

This had to be the *Agena*—the piece-of-junk *Agena*—causing exactly the kinds of trouble Lovell had warned them about. The smart move here was the one Lovell had recommended, and it actually involved two moves. Armstrong made them both.

First, he took hold of his attitude controller and used the thrusters on the *Gemini* to try to bring the two-ship assembly to heel. That worked—sort of—but the motion wasn't completely stilled.

So next he sent a command to the *Agena* to shut down its

guidance system completely. *Do nothing*, the manned spacecraft was ordering the unmanned one. *We'll take care of this.*

That seemed to do it. The two ships steadied themselves—but only for a moment. Then the erratic motion resumed. And then it accelerated, a full, three-axis tumble this time. Then it got faster still, which was extremely dangerous.

The worse the tumble became, the more centrifugal energy the two ships were generating, raising the possibility the *Agena* would simply rip away from the *Gemini*, tearing its metal skin and damaging the electronics, to say nothing of the parachutes, packed in the nose. If that happened, the astronauts could never come home.

What's more, the 4,000 pounds of explosive fuel in the *Agena*'s tanks had not gone anywhere. If the problem was being caused by an electrical glitch anywhere in the miles of cabling inside the ship, the possibility existed that it would ignite the tanks. *Gemini 8* had gone into a communications blackout from which it might never emerge.

The only way to save the crew was for Armstrong to hit the DISENGAGE switch, which would undock the two ships, flinging them away from one another. If the problem was a stuck thruster on the *Agena*—which it all but certainly was—he could stabilize his *Gemini*, make a quick jump to a higher orbit and leave it to NASA to command the *Agena* to make a suicide plunge into the atmosphere. With that bad-news spacecraft out of the way, he and Scott could go about the rest of their mission safely.

So Armstrong made that command decision, ordered Scott

to hit the switch that popped the latches and, as soon as that was done, fired a burst from his thrusters to back away fast from the *Agena*.

But the instability only grew worse—a lot worse. The *Gemini*'s tumble increased from a comparatively slow five revolutions per minute up to ten and then quickly to twenty.

Armstrong fought with his attitude controller while Scott threw breaker switches on the instrument panel in front of him, trying to see if the problem might be a bad thruster on the *Gemini*, rather than on the *Agena*. If it was, he could kill the power to that one jet and Armstrong could stabilize the ship with the ones remaining.

None of the breakers Scott tried had any effect, and the tumble increased to thirty RPMs.

"*Gemini 8*, communications check," came a voice in Armstrong's and Scott's headsets as they at last flew into range of the next tracking station, "how do you read?"

"We have serious problems here!" Scott answered. "We're tumbling end over end. We're disengaged from the *Agena*."

"What seems to be the problem?" the ground answered, either not understanding the severity of the emergency or trying too hard to sound calm.

"We're rolling and can't turn anything off," Armstrong said.

"We have a violent left roll," Scott added for emphasis.

That violent roll now increased to forty RPMs. The ground radioed back a "Roger, copy," but that was really all it could do.

Controllers on Earth could not override Armstrong's thruster maneuvers, and even if they could, they wouldn't. Only a pilot, in the seat, at the controls, feeling the motion as it happened, could respond fast enough to save this spacecraft.

Armstrong kept wrestling with his thrusters as Scott kept looking for a faulty breaker and the tumble increased to forty-five RPMs, then fifty and then fifty-five. They were closing in on sixty—or one revolution in multiple axes every second—and that would likely be the end.

Sixty RPMs was the point at which the integrity not only of the spacecraft would be threatened, but of the astronauts themselves. That was when even pilots who had spent count-less hours training in centrifuges would notice the first signs of vertigo setting in—the tunnel vision, the inability to orient, and finally the unconsciousness that would follow. With that, there would be no controlling force of any kind in charge of the spacecraft.

Already the dizziness was beginning and darkness was creeping in at the periphery of the astronauts' visual field.

Armstrong knew what he had to do.

"All we've got left is the reentry control system!" he shouted to Scott.

That might be the best answer, but it also came at a very high price.

Shutting down the main thrusters and going to the ones used during reentry was a one-way decision. The moment they did that, NASA rules decreed that they had to come home. They'd need the reentry thrusters to survive the plunge through the atmosphere at the end of the mission. If they used them now and then continued to fly for three more days, the fuel could clog and freeze the lines.

The mission, however, was no longer the thing that was on the line. The lives of the astronauts were.

"Press on!" Scott answered.

Armstrong did, killing his main thrusters, engaging his reentry system and slowly reducing the spin from deadly to serious, and finally back to manageable.

"We're regaining control of the spacecraft," Scott reported to the ground.

"Roger, copy," the ground responded.

And that, the ground didn't have to add, was that.

There would be no suite of experiments conducted. There would be no space walk—never mind two. Dave Scott would not become the man who walked around the world.

"I have some reentry data when you are ready to copy," the Hawaii tracking station said forlornly.

"Go ahead," Armstrong answered, revealing as little disappointment in his voice as he could.

Less than three hours after that—or only ten hours, forty-one minutes and twenty-six seconds into what was supposed to be a seventy-two-hour flight—*Gemini 8* splashed down in the Pacific Ocean.

NASA would later conclude that thruster number eight on the *Gemini* spacecraft had, as the engineers put it, failed open— it had switched itself on and nothing could turn it off.

The *Agena* had flown flawlessly. It was the *Gemini* that had gone wrong.

Three years and four months later, Neil Armstrong, survivor of Gemini 8, would serve as commander of *Apollo 11*, becoming the first human being to walk on the moon.

Two years after that, Dave Scott, the commander of *Apollo 15*, would become the seventh.

Gemini 8 might have been lost, but smart thinking by its crew allowed later history to be made.